# THE ADVENTUROUS GIRL'S HANDBOOK

# THE ADVENTUROUS GIRL'S HANDBOOK

## For Ages 9 to 99

Edited by
Stephen Brennan and Lara Brennan

Skyhorse Publishing

Skyhorse Publishing books may be purchased in bulk at special discounts for sales promotion, corporate gifts, fund-raising, or educational purposes. Special editions can also be created to specifications. For details, contact the Special Sales Department, Skyhorse Publishing, 555 Eighth Avenue, Suite 903, New York, NY 10018 or info@ skyhorsepublishing.com.

www.skyhorsepublishing.com

10 9 8 7 6 5 4 3 2 1

Library of Congress Cataloging-in-Publication Data

Brennan, Steve, 1952-
    The adventurous girl's handbook : for ages 9 to 99 / Stephen Brennan and Lara Brennan.
        p. cm.
    Includes bibliographical references.
    ISBN 978-1-60239-635-7
    1. Handicraft for girls. 2. Recreation. 3. Girls--Miscellanea. I. Brennan, Lara, 1996- II. Title.
    TT171.B74 2009
    745.5--dc22
                                2009009138

Printed in China

*With much love*
*to Mari Lyons, Mother,*
*Grandmother, Artist, Adventurous Girl.*

# ACKNOWLEDGMENTS

Many thanks to Tony Lyons and Bill Wolfsthal at Skyhorse Publishing for seeing the possibilities of this book. Also to Ann Treistman, our crack editor, for all her guidance and leadership.

Many thanks also to Steve Corcoran for his tireless work in helping us to assemble this book.

# CONTENTS

## NATURE

## APPENDIX

# INTRODUCTION

*"These days a girl takes her adventure where she can get it."*

What a terrific idea it was to do this book with my daughter. How often do you get to spend that kind of focused and productive time with any member of your family—much less your eldest and the apple of your eye? I have to admit that at the start of our work together I had some vague notion or idea that this would be largely a teaching process—you know, the wise old dad shows his little girl the ins and outs of putting together a book. He expects that he will have to do most of the work and that she will write her entries and then deliver them, piecemeal and half-baked, when he can whip her to it. But it hasn't worked out that way at all. I can tell you that Lara had been a full partner in the compiling, writing, and editing of this *Adventurous Girl's Handbook*. Our modus was to laugh a lot and argue just a little, and thereby help both to check and stimulate the other's interests and excesses. As we neared the end of our labors I asked her whether or not she was glad she had taken this on.

"Glad," she said, displaying what is for her a rare economy of words.

"Very glad?" I prompted.

"Yes," she said smiling, "very glad."

I was glad of it too. And truth to tell, I felt some need of gladdening. Only a few weeks earlier a day had come that every father dreads. It was early morning and I was walking Lara to school, as had been my wont since her preschool days, when she turned to me and said, "I don't want you to walk me to school anymore."

"But," I said, "I've always walked you."

"I want to go by myself."

"You're too young to walk alone to school," I said.

"I'll meet up with my friends and we'll go together. Don't you trust me?"

"It's not a matter of trust." I said. "It isn't safe."

"I'll be careful," she said, as if that settled the matter. I noticed that down the block two of her classmates appeared to be waiting for her to join them.

"Sorry Lara, I don't think it's a good idea," I said.

"Dad, I'm old enough. If you insist, you can follow me to school, but you have to walk at least a block behind me. Honestly, it'll be fine." With that she waved, gave a shout, and, taking off after her friends, called back at me, "It'll be an adventure!"

This question of what adventure is was much on my mind as we began working together on this book, and one day I put the question directly to my coauthor.

"Oh Lara."

"Yes dad?"

"What is an adventure?"

"Dad, you are asking the wrong question."

"Am I?"

"Oh my god, yes. The important question is not 'What is an adventure?' Everybody knows that. The really interesting question is 'What does it mean to be adventurous?'"

That insight has served as the keynote for this book. Our aim has been to make a compilation that gives the Adventurous Girl access to things that may help to grow adventurousness in her. It may be an adventure to rappel off a cliff face or down a mountain side, but the adventurous girl is one who wishes to and imagines herself undertaking that danger, whether she ever gets the opportunity or not. It may be an even greater adventure to save a life and the adventurous girl is prepared to act should the need arise.

In the closing decades of the 19th century, with the industrialization of printing, began what we have to consider as a "golden age" of books for young people—not only for boys but for girls as well. This was the era of the great girl novels: of *Black Beauty* by Anna Sewall for example, or *Little Women* by Louisa May Alcott, or *Alice In Wonderland* by Lewis Carroll, or *Silas Marner* by George Eliot. By the turn of the century, and thanks largely to public education, a majority of high-school-aged Americans were able to read. This was great news for the publishing industry and for American literature. This was also the era of the sequel and the prequel and all the other little quels. In 1917, Eleanor H. Porter's *Pollyanna* was such a runaway bestseller that Ms. Porter was encouraged to write eleven more follow-on books. *Heidi,* by the Swiss writer Johanna Spyri, proved to be such a favorite year in and year out that its English translator took it upon himself to write two sequels: *Heidi Grows Up* and *Heidi's Children.* Whole syndicates sprang up, devoted to feeding the market with adventure stories for girls. In 1930 the first four Nancy Drew Mysteries were published. Since then over eighty million Nancy Drew books have been sold.

Nonfiction works for girls were also a big deal. At first the books tended to be how-to books centered on home crafts, like cooking and sewing, and on the genteel arts of hand-stitched embroidery, water-color painting, and music, or on the finer points of bourgeois etiquette. However, this soon changed. In 1913 George Bernard Shaw was heard to lament that "home is the girl's prison." But already girls all over the Western world were breaking free. In America, the popular market was already aflood with memoirs and truelife adventures of women in sports and in the arts. The rise of scouting, for both boys and girls, did a great deal to make available a life out of doors, and even the early Scout Manuals somehow manage to be the last word on the woodcraft, the flora, and the fauna of the natural world.

There's something about the flowering of this genre that is still mighty attractive, and so for our book we have consciously chosen to reflect these traditions by excerpting works from several of the masters. Di Souza was a master horseman and teacher, nevermind his quaint way of expressing himself. The work of Ernest Thompson Seton, who helped found the Scouting Movement (for boys and girls) in America, is very good on woodcraft and the outdoors—the natural world, and was an important resource. Eloise Roorbach was an athlete, hiker, and mountain-climbing naturalist in the early days of the 20th century, when this kind of triple or quadruple threat was rare. But not all of our contributors are graybeards. Most of this material is as up-to-date as anyone could wish. A number of entries have been written by friends and, in a couple cases, classmates. Some of our information has been gleaned from the Web. In rendering this material, we've tried wherever possible for an easy, off-handed, avuncular approach, one that fully respects the information we want to get across but does so in a voice that maximizes it accessibility.

The other day I was to meet up with Lara after school. We'd fixed our rendezvous for a particular street corner, but I was early and it was drizzly out so I ducked into a coffee shop. The windows gave a good view of the corner so I'd be able to watch for her from there and keep myself dry. A few moments later I was surprised to see not Lara only but a whole posse of her classmates stride into my ken. There were no adults with them and they had not seen me. Most of them had known one another since kindergarten and there was an ease between them and a goodnatured jocularity. Sure each of them was her own person with her own qualities and traits—one awkward, another blasé, one earnest, another preoccupied. But taken together, they were a revelation. It seemed to me a true vision of Girl Power. And a voice in my head said, "Glass ceilings, you better look out, these girls are fit for any adventure."

Stephen Brennan
Lara Brennan
March 2009

# ARTS AND CRAFTS

## MODELING IN CLAY

An eminent artist once remarked that, should he bring into his studio the first dozen boys he happened to meet on the street, taking them as they came, he would probably be able to teach at least half of them to model within six months, whereas there might not be one of them who could be taught to paint at all. Possibly none of these boys would ever become great sculptors, but they could learn to model moderately well. If that is the case with boys, who are apt to be so awkward and clumsy, how quickly could a girl's deft fingers learn to mold and form the plastic clay into lifelike forms?

The great difficulty we encounter in learning to draw—which is representing things as they appear, not as they really are—will not trouble us in this other department of art, for in modeling it must be our aim to do precisely the reverse and reproduce an object exactly *as it is*, not as it appears.

Modeling, besides its own worth, is of value as an aid to drawing for it teaches form, and the shadows on an object can be drawn more intelligently and correctly when it is known just what formations produce them.

Instead of entering into the finished processes, we will confine ourselves to the prelude or introduction to modeling; and then, girls, with the object before you—your only guide and instructor—you must work out the rest for yourselves.

### MATERIALS

Clay, such as is used by potters, perfectly free from grit.

Modeling tools. These can be bought at any artists' material store, and the simplest ones might be made at home of hard wood. Only a few tools are necessary for a beginner; the fingers and thumbs are the best of all tools, and a great deal can be done with them, though for fine, delicate modeling, tools must be used.

Modeling stand. A regular modeling stand with rotary platform will cost a little money, and the expense may be an objection; but an ordinary high office stool with revolving seat makes a good substitute. If the stool is not high enough, it can be raised by placing a drawing- or pastry-board, on the seat and on top of that a square wooden box about one foot high and broad enough to allow sufficient room for a good-sized head and bust.

## HOW TO MANAGE CLAY

To begin with, about fifty pounds of modeling clay will be required. If possible buy it moist, but if its dry, put it into an earthenware jar, or anything that will hold water, and cover with clear water. Let it remain until thoroughly moistened then, with a stick, stir the clay around until it is free from lumps and is perfectly smooth. Clear it away from the sides of the jar and pile it up in the center.

When the clay is dry enough not to be muddy but still pliable, it is in a fit condition to work with. It is necessary to keep your hands perfectly clean and conveniences for washing them should be handy.

Do not use muddy water or a dusty towel.

Use any tools that will produce the desired result with the greatest ease; a little experience will soon determine what these tools are but as a rule the largest are best.

When leaving unfinished work, cover it with a damp cloth to keep it moist.

If you are working on a head, and the features have been started, stick a small wooden tool in the head just above the forehead to hold the cloth away from the face, for it is liable to soften the nose and push it out of shape if it rests upon it.

Keep your tools clean, and do not allow the metal ones to become rusty, as they will if carelessly left on the modeling stand when not in use. To avoid trouble of this kind it is best to put your tools in a box where they will be perfectly dry.

## HOW TO PRESERVE MODELED CLAY

If terracotta clay is used, it can be baked in a kiln, which will, while hardening, turn it a fine buff terracotta color and make the object, if well modeled, ornamental enough for almost any use.

From the other clay, plaster casts can be taken and the article can be reproduced in plaster as many times as desired.

## HINTS FOR MODELING A HEAD

Always work from a model, and it is best to try copying plaster casts before attempting to model from life.

Place a wooden or tin box (something the size of a cigar box will do) on the center of your stand to form the base; cover this with clay and stick a support in the middle.

The support may be a piece of doll or even kindling wood eight inches long and about one inch thick.

Build up the clay around this stick and, with your hands, mold the clay, piecing it out here and cutting off there, until it bears some resemblance to a head.

Still using your hands, get the general proportions of the head and then begin on the features. Begin with the profile, using tools when necessary, and try for character without detail; then turn the head a little and work from that point of view. Always look at your model from the same point of view as you do your work. Turn the head in the opposite direction and model the other side, keeping the face evenly balanced. Continue turning your work little by little until each outline it presents is as near as you can get to the corresponding outline of your model, and then work up the detail.

In modeling any object, the same process of viewing the model from all points, must be done.

Do not strive to obtain a likeness at first, but be careful to have all of your outlines correct, and the likeness will come by itself.

## SEWING

It used to be that most girls learned to sew by hand. This was regarded not just as a domestic accomplishment but also an art. These days we mostly buy our clothes ready-made and it seems with every generation, fewer and fewer of us practice this craft or art. This is too bad because there really is a kind of magic in the nimble fingers of an accomplished seamstress.

## SEVERAL STITCHES

From *School Needlework* by Olive C. Hapgood:

STITCHING

BACKSTITCHING

RIGHT SIDE

WRONG SIDE

*HEMMING*

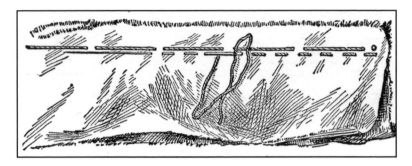

RUNNING

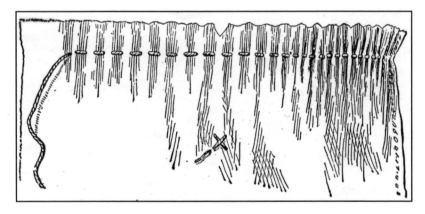

GATHERING

## ROPES

From the very dawn of human intelligence, people have found it necessary to fasten things together. Vines, tree bark, branches, as well as strips of animal hides and leather have all served us, at one time or another, in our history.

Rope, cord, twine, and even thread are our more modern means to the same end.

All sewing is dependent upon threads and cloth is merely groups of such threads woven together.

These are made from fibers found in the leaves or stems of plants, or from animal wools.

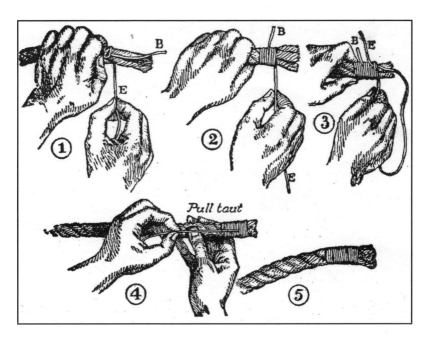

Common hemp is the fiber most often used for rope, though cotton ropes are more flexible and very durable. Manilla hemp is used for stiff, heavy ropes.

When the fibers have been combed out of the leaves the following steps occur:

A few **fibers** are twisted together to the **right** to form **yarn**. Then a few **yarns** are twisted together to the **left** to form a **strand**.

Three **strands** are twisted together to the **right** to form a **hawser; hawsers** are twisted together to the **left** to form a **cable**.

A one inch rope may have as many as 300 individual threads and the friction of each against the others gives holding strength to the rope.

Take a small piece of string and separate it back as far as you can toward its fibers. The nature of the rope, then, is such that its ends will fray or separate and gradually unravel.

It is important, therefore, to "whip" the ends of your rope.

## "WHIPPING" A ROPE

The idea is to "bury" the two ends so they are held by the other loops. After making several turns, the end can be pulled tight under those turns and cut off.

## A FEW REALLY USEFUL KNOTS

To use ropes and cords one must know how to make them **hold**. Knots, therefore, are in constant use by sailors, explorers, mountain climbers, engineers, and mechanics.

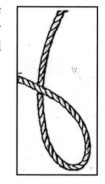

A good knot has three qualities:

> It can be **tied quickly**.
> It will **hold fast**.
> It can be **easily untied**.

When tying a rope there are three parts:

> **The standing part**—the long unused portion.
> **The Bight**—the loop formed whenever the rope is turned back
> **The End**—the part used in leading

### THE FIGURE-OF-EIGHT KNOT

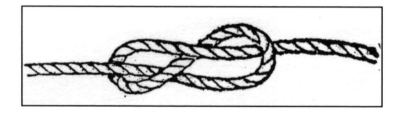

### THE OVERHAND KNOT

These may be used to keep a rope from "pulling through" a pulley or an opening as in the case of a shoelace.

### SQUARE OR REEF

The most common knot for tying two ropes together, frequently used in first-aid bandaging. It never slips or jams and is easy to untie.

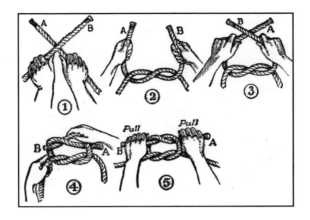

*SHEET BEND*

This knot is used in bending the sheet to the clew of a sail and in tying two rope-ends together.

*THE BOWLINE*

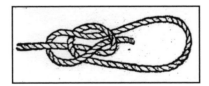

A noose that neither jams nor slips. Used in lowering a person from a burning building, etc.

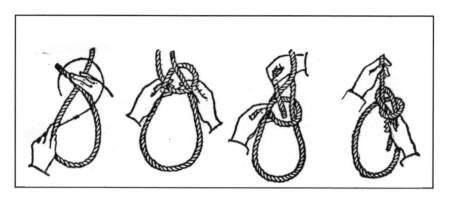

HOW TO TIE THE BOWLINE

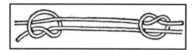

### THE FISHERMAN'S KNOT

Used for tying silk gut for fishing purposes. It never slips and is easily unloosed by pulling the two short ends.

### SHEEPSHANK

Used for shortening ropes. Gather up the amount to be shortened then make a half hitch around each of the bends.

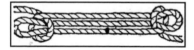

### SLIP, OR RUNNING, KNOT

The harder this knot is pulled, the tighter its loop becomes.

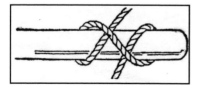

### CLOVE HITCH

Used to fasten one pole to another in fitting up scaffolding; this knot holds snugly and is not likely to slip laterally.

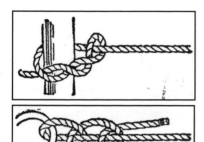

### TIMBER HITCH

Used in hauling timber.

### TWO HALF HITCHES

Useful because they are easily made and will not slip under any strain.

### ROPE HALTERS

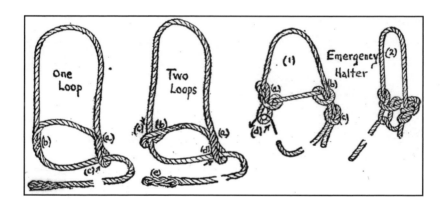

### HITCHING TIE

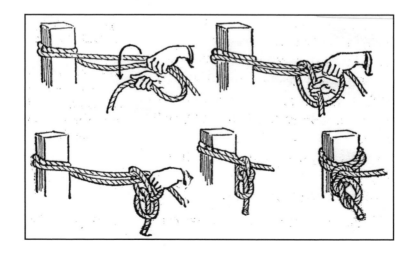

## PRESSED FLOWERS

Although these are perfectly flat, they seldom fade and are very pretty and useful. Have ready a large book or a quantity of old newspapers and several weights when pressing flowers. Use the newspapers for leaves and ferns—blotting paper is best for the flowers. Both the flowers and leaves should be fresh and without moisture. Place them as nearly in their natural positions as possible in the book or papers and press, allowing several thicknesses of paper between each layer. Move the specimens onto dry papers each day until perfectly dry.

Some flowers must be immersed—all but the flower head—in boiling water for a few minutes before pressing, to prevent them from turning black. Orchids are of this nature.

If possible, it is best to obtain all parts of a plant, the roots as well as the seeds, for a more interesting collection can thus be made than from just the flower and leaf alone.

It is advisable to be provided with a blank book or, what is still better, pieces of stiff white paper of uniform size on which to mount the flowers or leaves when dried; also you'll need a small bottle of mucilage and a brush for fastening them, and some narrow strips of court-plaster or gummed paper for the stems and thicker parts of the plants. The sooner they can be mounted, the better. Place them carefully on the paper, writing beneath the locality and date of finding. Flowers and leaves thus prepared make beautiful herbariums.

## HOW TO DRAW

*By Frank Beard*

Would you like to learn to draw, to sketch from nature? Don't you think that it would be great to be able to take out your pencils and paper and copy some scene you want to remember, or produce a likeness of anything which strikes your fancy?

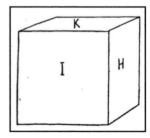

Many will say, "I'd like it, but I *can't* draw."

You can write, can hold a pencil, and can trace lines upon the paper; and if you can do this, you can draw a little. A girl who can learn anything can learn to draw if she will

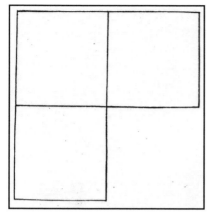

give the same attention to it that she gives to other things.

Now we are not going to talk about copying pictures which someone else has already drawn, for there is not much satisfaction in making imitations of other people's work; it is much more gratifying to make the original drawings ourselves but to do this we need some direction.

The reason it is easier to copy a picture than to draw the real object is because the lines to be copied are all laid out on the flat surface of the picture; but to draw an object we must find out where to trace the lines for ourselves.

For instance, suppose we are to draw a flowerpot and plant. If we have the picture before us, we can readily see where all the lines are placed upon the paper, but in viewing a real plant and pot we are apt to become confused in trying to discover the directions and proportions of the lines.

Therefore we must learn *to see things as they appear*, not as they really are. This may seem strange to you, because one is apt to think that a thing must appear as it is; but let us look into the matter.

We will take a square box. Now, we know that all the sides are the same size, that the top is as large as the side, and that one side is as large as another. But if you try to draw it so, you will find it impossible because, although you know that the top and sides are the same size as the front, they do not look so and you draw things as they look, not as they really are.

Take this example. We all know that a man's leg is longer than his arm, but it doesn't always appear so. Measure the arms and legs of the man pictured here, and you will see by actual measurement the arms are longer than the legs, and yet it looks right because the legs are projected toward you; in other words, the legs are *fore-shortened*.

The great secret of drawing from nature is to train the eye to see a real object just like a picture.

Now let us return to our flowerpot again. We will suppose we are drawing from a real flowerpot and plant. We determine how large we will make our sketch and begin operations by drawing a vertical line (a straight, upright line). Along this line we will mark out the proportions of the plant and pot.

We may easily discover that the plant is longer than the pot. This can be done by holding the pencil upright before the eye at arm's length, so that it will cover the pot, and by measuring with the thumb the height of the pot, raising the arm so as to cover the plant, and comparing the measurement of the pot with the plant. The lines drawn from the eye show how the pencil takes the measurement on the object.

After settling the question of the height of the flowerpot and plant, we will mark the measurements on the line. And now we will draw in the pot, leaving the straight line through its center.

On observing the plant we will see that it is not exactly straight, and here again the straight line will be of assistance.

By holding up our pencil, which represents the straight line, we will discover that the main stem of the plant leans considerably to the left. Guided by the line, we can get the curve of the stem about right. Now we sketch the stem. Along the straight line we again measure the distance from the top of each leaf and flower to the pot. We can see several leaves, each reaching a certain height. Observing the same plan of mea-

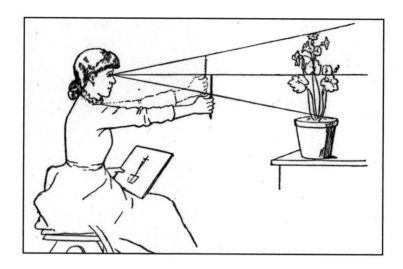

surement, we find that the top of the lowest leaf is about the same height from the pot as the height of the pot itself and again, from the top of the lowest leaf to the top of the plant measures the same distance.

By drawing another vertical line just touching the right side of the pot, we find that it touches the extreme edge of the leaf. Thus we find the exact situation as the leaf. By the same method we find the right places for the other leaves and flowers, and after we know just where they belong, we draw them in and find that we have produced a very creditable outline from nature.

We need not confine ourselves to one or two guiding lines in sketching an object; in fact, we may use as many straight lines as will help us to get the correct proportions—not only vertical and horizontal lines but slanting lines will also assist us in most cases.

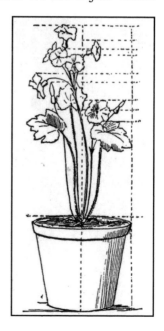

The sketch of a dog will give a clear idea of the way to employ all lines necessary in sketching from nature. A few words will be all that is necessary to explain this illustration.

There lies the dog on the floor, and we seat ourselves at a little distance from it with pencil and paper. We will start off with a hor-izontal line (A); then we can form some idea as to whether the little dog lies along a straight line or not and, in case the bottom line slants, how much it slants. Then draw the vertical line (BE). Now suppose we hold our pencil upright, in such a position as to touch the back of the knee joint of the dog's foreleg, we will find that it passes through the middle of the dog's back, as represented by the line (BE); so we have found the correct places for these parts.

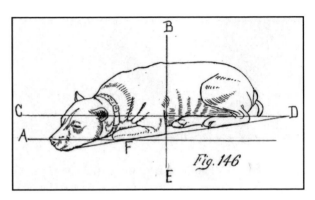

Fig. 146

Another horizontal line (CD) drawn above the first will touch just over the right eye, pass through the middle of the left ear, through the middle of the neck, cut off the foreleg, and run along the top of the two hind legs, passing through the knee of the left side. This will show us that the top of the right eye, the ear, and the top of both hind legs are on a line. It will also help us to get the proportions above and below the line. Then by drawing a line from D to the point F on the horizontal line A, we find that the lower edges of the left hind and fore legs are on the same line, which, if extended a little farther down, will touch the edge of the dog's mouth. With these lines to guide us we cannot go astray in our proportions.

In beginning the practice of drawing from nature, we had better confine our first efforts to things that will stand still, for without a practiced hand it will be almost impossible to sketch a restless subject; but if we attempt to do so, we should follow the example methods below as closely as possible.

Now, suppose we step out of doors in search of something to sketch. The first moving object our eyes rest upon is a goose, and we decide to use him as a model.

But he is so restless and will not keep still for an instant. First, we have a front view, then a side view, and again he turns his back on us. If we really must have his drawing, the only way is to catch him and tie him up.

Yet even now he is a difficult subject, twisting and turning, and bobbing his head about. Determined to sketch him, however, we observe the position in which he remains the longest time, or assumes most often, and begin our work.

We first note the general proportions. Is his body as thick as it is long? Is his neck as long as his body? Are his legs nearest the head or tail? Is the head as long as the neck? What part reaches the highest or what part the lowest? We hastily but carefully consider these questions and determine in our own mind the answers, for we must get an idea of the proportions before we begin our sketch.

Now we draw a horizontal line along our paper and then hold up our pencil horizontally, so that it will answer for a straight line drawn across the body of the real goose.

This will represent the horizontal line on the paper. Noticing then the directions the outlines of the goose take from the horizontal line (represented by the pencil), we sketch them in on the paper, remembering that one of the most important things is to get the right directions of the lines.

Observe that the line G is directed at too high a point and makes the body too thick and out of proportion.

In sketching it is best to make all lines straight instead of curves, for in this way we are more likely to get the right directions. Our first rough sketch of the goose ought to have something of the appearance of our last example, and as we work on it more carefully it will become as nicely rounded as we could desire.

One of the most common faults a beginner is apt to have is to try to do too much, either by choosing too great a subject, such as a large landscape, or by putting too many little things into the composition. Take care of the large things, and the little things will take care of themselves.

If our subject is a clump of trees at some distance, we should not attempt to draw in separate leaves but endeavor to get the true shape of the tree, simply indicating the leaves by a few lines. Nor must we

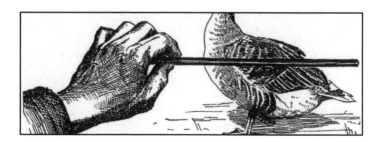

attempt, in our first sketches, to put in all the shadows we see; the strong principal ones are all that are necessary. A background of hills and trees should be merely suggested by a few lines, because the light striking upon them gives a very light appearance.

Draw as simply as possible. Ten pictures are spoiled by putting in too much work while one is spoiled by too little.

Don't be discouraged. Every effort will show improvement, if you really put your mind and heart in to your work.

## MATERIALS

A sheet of drawing-paper, a No. 2 pencil, and an eraser are all you really need in order to commence. Later it will be beneficial to have a drawing-pad and several more pencils.

## HOW TO PAINT IN WATERCOLORS

There is a certain charm in watercolor painting—a charm distinctly its own—which lies, as Penley says, "in the beauty and truthfulness of its aerial tones." Without this quality a watercolor, as a watercolor, is a failure.

This transparency of effect does not depend alone upon the manner of painting or the colors employed but rests largely with the paper we use. In the days when our mothers and grandmothers were taught painting at school, the finest, smoothest cardboard was thought necessary; we have since learned that flat, smooth paper decidedly produces a flat, smooth effect in the picture painted upon it, while rough, uneven surfaces of the paper now used helps to produce depth and atmosphere. Therefore it is best to have *rough* paper to paint upon.

## MATERIALS FOR WATERCOLOR PAINTING

Rough drawing or watercolor paper.

### BRUSHES

The best brushes are made of sable, and although costing more to begin with, it is really more economical to purchase them than to choose the less-expensive camel-hair brush. The sable are by far the most satisfactory and will last much longer. Three or four brushes are sufficient.

### COLORS

A box of moist colors, which also contains a palette, is very useful but the colors can be bought separately in tubes or pans.

Watercolor painting seems, by its qualities, to be especially adapted to flowers and landscapes, so we will confine ourselves to the principal points to be observed in these two subjects.

### FLOWERS

Few oil paintings, however well executed, give the delicate, exquisite texture of a flower as nearly as watercolors. The semi-transparency of a rose petal, and the juicy, translucent green of a young leaf is difficult to accurately represent in anything other than these paints, whose essential quality is transparency. To preserve this transparency of color, everything about the painting must be kept exceedingly neat. The brushes must be thoroughly washed before using them, for a different tint from a previously used color could be on them, and plenty of water, changed frequently, is necessary.

Having conveniently arranged your materials, place your paper so that it will lie at an angle slanting toward you, not perfectly flat upon the table; this can be done by putting books under the edge farthest from you, thus raising it up. Stand the flowers you wish to copy in such a position that the light will fall upon them only from one direction and produce decided shadows; the effect will then be much better than if the light is more diffused.

Always arrange your model exactly as you want to paint it and leave nothing to the imagination. If you do not intend to have any background other than the white paper, place something white behind your flowers. If you want a colored background, arrange the color you have chosen behind the flowers and paint it as you see it. Commence your work by sketching lightly, as correctly and rapidly as you can, the outline of your flower. Try something simple at first; say a bunch of heartsease or pansies, and when drawing try to get the character of both flower and leaf. Observe how the stem curves where it is attached to the flower and at what angles the stems of the flowers and the leaves join the main stalk.

When your outline is drawn, dip your largest brush in clear water and go over the whole surface of your paper; then place a piece of blotting paper over the paper to soak up the water, leaving it simply damp, not wet.

If you are using tube colors, have ready on a palette, or ordinary dinner plate, these colors: crimson lake, cobalt blue, indigo, Prussian blue, and gamboge. Put in your lightest tints first, leaving the white paper for the highest light; then paint in your darker tints and shadows, and get the desired effect.

If your flower is what we call the "johnny-jump-up," the lowest petal will be yellow. Paint this in with a light wash of gamboge, leaving, as we have said, the white paper for touches of high light. The two upper petals will probably be a deep-claret color; this is made by mixing crimson lake and cobalt blue, the crimson lake dominating. The two central petals may be a bluish lavender, and this color is made by mixing a little crimson lake with cobalt blue. Use plenty of water, but do not let it run, and keep the colors of the petals distinct.

Paint the stems and leaves, where they are a rich green, with a mixture of gamboge and Prussian blue, and where they appear gray as the light touches them, a pale wash of indigo will give the desired effect.

Keep your shadows broad and distinct and your tints as flat as you can. Leave out details altogether in your first paintings and add them afterward only when you can do so without spoiling the effect.

When a tinted background is desired, put it in quickly in a flat tint, before commencing the flowers. It is best not to bring the tint quite up to the outline, as a narrow edge of white left around the flower gives a pleasant, sketchy look to the painting.

## LANDSCAPES

In your first studies from nature keep to simple subjects and treat them simply, without any attempt at elaboration.

The process of laying on color and lightly washing over them afterward should be repeated several times, and the result will be a transparent aerial tone.

Keep your extreme distance bluish, your middle distance warmer in tone but not too strong, and the principal objects in your foreground strong.

Leave out small objects and with light and shade seek to obtain the overall effect.

Keep your colors pure or your sketch will be dull.

Contrast has much to do in producing strength and character in your watercolor.

## BEADWORK

Making beadwork on a loom is a fascinating occupation and when the large beads are used the work grows quickly. However, it is wiser to use the small beads as the results will produce much finer work. It is easy to make one's own design on cross-stitch paper, and the design below was done by a girl of twelve. It is the beginning of a belt that is intended to give the principal "milestones" in the life of the wearer. Another girl made a belt of one summer's experiences—her favorite canoe, the island where she stayed, etc.

## THE USE OF THE BEAD LOOM

### *TO SET UP THE LOOM*

1. Decide how many beads will be used to make the proper width. Cut off one more thread than the number of beads (in the width) to be used. For example, if there are to be nine beads cut off ten threads.
2. The threads should be somewhat longer than the strip of beadwork is intended to be when finished.
3. Fasten all the ends neatly to the tack or pin on the roller.
4. Place each thread separately in a groove and draw smoothly over to the opposite groove and fasten to the peg.

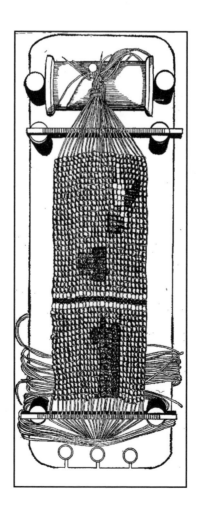

## TO BEGIN THE BEADWORK

1. Thread needle with long thread.
2. Fasten end securely on lowest thread, with the spool of loom on the left-hand side.
3. On the needle pick up the required number of beads (one less than the total number of strings) arranged in color so as to make the design you have sketched.
4. Slip the beads on to the end of thread and pass them under the threads to the top. Press the beads into place, one between each two threads.
5. Hold the beads with your left hand, while passing the needle back through them from the top, making sure that the thread goes from under the top thread over it and back into the top bead.

## THE BEGINNING OF A BEAD BELT

### TOP VIEW OF BEAD LOOM

The first picture represents birth. A stork carrying a basket with the baby's head is shown flying to a house.

The second represents a journey to Canada. A train and car are followed by an arrow pointing to a land of pine trees in snow.

# SPORTS

## SWIMMING AND LIFE SAVING

If you learn to swim well you have a sense of independence and assurance that goes far toward developing the poise and self-reliance so helpful to future success. The self-confidence that comes from mastering the art of swimming helps to make every new task easier. Swimming is exceeded by no other exercise in the development of a healthy body and physical grace. As a play-place, the swimming pool is unequalled.

### PARTNERS

*The Buddy Plan.* The first rule in swimming is to always swim with others. Swimmers are usually paired off according to their ability to swim and stay together both in shallow water and deep water. During the entire swimming period, partners, or "buddies," stay together, never out of sight of each other, and they leave the water together.

Do not try to learn to swim alone. Always work in the water with a teacher. The teacher may be your swimming partner, but do not go into the water alone.

### MAIN POINTS IN LEARNING TO SWIM

Four things, none of them difficult in themselves, must be mastered:

Correct breathing
Balance
Relaxation
Correct motion

## BREATHING

Correct breathing while in the water is quite opposite to ordinary breathing. In ordinary breathing you take the air in through the nose; but in the water, you inhale through the mouth above water, in order that you may take the air in more quickly, and you exhale slowly through the nose underwater, or nose and partly closed lips, so that you may keep the nose passages free of water.

You can easily learn to breathe correctly at home, using any deep basin or a large bowl. Fill the basin two-thirds full of water, lean forward, place your hands on your knees, and hold your face just above the water. Take a deep breath through your open mouth; close your mouth and expel the air through the nose, which should be close to but not quite touching the water. Watch the ripples the expelled air makes on the water's surface.

Repeat this a number of times, until you become accustomed to this new style of breathing.

Next, as you exhale, lower your face—eyes, nose, and mouth—into the water and blow bubbles. Withdraw your face before your breath is exhausted, to prevent water from getting into the nose, as it would if you stopped blowing before raising your head. Repeat this until your breathing is easy and evenly timed.

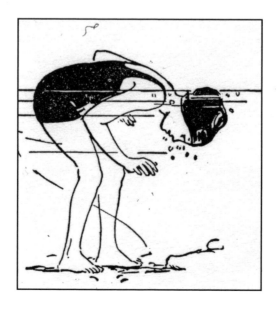

The next step is to keep your head level and turn your face up for air, as you will do when swimming, instead of taking your head out of the water entirely, as you have been doing.

The proper movement of the legs and arms may also be practiced at home. The knack of relaxation and the skill of balance, however, can be acquired only in the water with a swimming partner and the swimming teacher at hand.

## BALANCE

Balance means that you are so nicely poised in the water that you are able to stay up and move forward easily.

## RELAXATION

Relaxation means to "let go," that is, to loosen up your muscles so that you will not become exhausted and can balance and float easily and swim long distances without fatigue. To get the best idea of relaxation, lie down flat on the floor and then try to "let go" so much that you are even flatter—completely relaxed.

### Floating

*Face-Floating.* Your instructor will probably teach you to float in waist-deep water. Floating should be easy if you have already become used to having your face in the water and are able to relax. Of course, your partner will help you if you need help, and you, in turn, will help your partner. Before practicing the float without support, you must learn to regain a standing position.

Before trying another float position be sure that you know how to regain your feet in shallow water without ducking and choking. Slowly

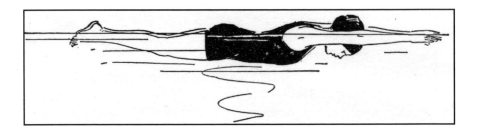

raise your head out of the water; bend your knees until they nearly touch your chest; bear down on the water with your hands, place your feet on the bottom of the pool far apart, knees relaxed until you can balance, then straighten your legs and stand.

*Floating on Your Back.* Squat in the water to submerge your shoulders and incline your body backward until your head is in the water with your ears under water; raise your hips slowly and push off from the bottom. Extend your body in the water, keeping yourself well-relaxed. Your arms should be stretched sideways, with the palms on the water. Before practicing this float without support, learn to regain a standing position.

*To Regain Standing Position from Back-Floating.* Bend your knees and sink the hips, as in a sitting position. Bend your head forward—downward toward your knees; move your arms backward from their outstretched position, then, making a quick energetic scoop forward-downward by the sides of your body, finish with the palms up well forward (as if holding a book to read). As you place your feet on the bottom of the pool far apart, knees relaxed to balance, straighten your legs to a standing position.

## CORRECT MOTION

*The Crawl.* When the floating positions have been mastered, the next thing to learn will be the crawl stroke.

The crawl leg stroke, which is usually learned first, is a series of down and up kicks with the feet, toes turned in, "pigeon-toed," and legs straight from hips to relaxed ankles. Try this lying face down on a stool or chair. Let the feet pass close together, the greatest distance between the upper foot and the lower one ranging from eight to twelve inches. Try this leg action also lying flat on your back, with feet raised slightly so that you can see them. Remember to keep the ankles loose and toes turned in. Start foot action slowly as it is easier to relax when moving slowly.

The arm stroke may be practiced while standing in front of a mirror. Each arm acts like a paddle that is propelling a canoe. One at a time the hands are extended forward and down and pulled back nearly to the knee and then slowly reached forward for the next stroke.

One arm is, of course, half a circle ahead of the other, so that one is always pulling while the other is moving forward.

There are two points to remember about this arm stroke: first, that the pull is backward and under the body; and second, that as the arm is lifted and moves forward, the elbow is slightly raised, so that it would be above the surface if you were in the water. After practicing the crawl on land you may practice it at the swimming pool, working with your partner and your teacher in shallow water. Add the arm and leg strokes to the face-floating position, and, when this is well learned, try timing

proper breathing with the arm stroke. Turn your face up for air as you reach forward, getting your breath through your mouth, and then letting it out underwater through your nose. After faithful practice all these steps that may have seemed individually awkward will combine, and you will be able to swim.

*Treading Water.* Every swimmer should be able to tread water, using the frog or scissors kick, in slow rhythm, keeping head and hands above the surface for at least thirty seconds. Some find a modification of a bicycle pedaling motion of the feet effective, emphasizing the downward strokes of the soles of the feet.

After you have learned to swim, you may then learn different swimming strokes and how to dive. You should learn to swim on your back, for it relaxes you when you are tired and may sometime be the means to saving your life in water.

## LIFE SAVING

If an Adventurous Girl is thoroughly practiced in methods of helping persons in distress in the water, with boat, lifebuoy, or by swimming, she may some day put her ability to use.

In case of a water accident she can best assist a person in trouble by calling for help and then trying to place some sort of float—a lifebuoy or a rope, a board, or even a tree branch—in the hands of the drowning person; or, if there is a boat close at hand, she may row the boat to the victim and permit her to hold on to the stern (back end) of the boat until safety is reached.

Perfect yourself in your swimming so that, in case of need, you can safely take care of yourself, leaving the person who might have tried to help you free to save someone else.

## SAVE YOURSELF

Before attempting to rescue another person from the water by swimming, you must be fully competent to take care of yourself in the water. It is especially important to understand the value of floating, for you may sometime find yourself in water either too rough for swimming or so far from shore that swimming will do you little good.

## UNDRESSING IN THE WATER

If you should be thrown suddenly into the water with all your clothes on and must swim ashore in order to save your life, remove all clothing as follows:

During the process of undressing, come up and take a good breath whenever needed. Lay your face in the water so you can see your shoes, then unlace and remove them. Loosen your blouse or coat so it can be removed and you can get it up under your arms so that by crossing hands you can pull it over your head as you duck under.

If, however, you can be saved only by floating and remaining quietly in the water, it is better to leave all clothing on except your shoes, as clothing is buoyant for a certain length of time and also contains a certain amount of warmth, even though wet.

If you are not buoyant and cannot float, you should tread water and scull gently enough to keep afloat until help comes.

## SAVE ANOTHER

In attempting the rescue of another person, remember that swimming is the last method of rescue to be used and not the first, and is to be resorted to only when other means are not practicable.

The Adventurous Girl should keep the following points in mind:

Practically all drowning accidents occur within a few feet of shallow water, or from a wharf or solid structure which offers support.

Over 50 percent of the persons who go down have some swimming ability and usually need some simple assistance such as a push toward shore to help to get them into a swimming position from the standing position in which they struggle.

The first thing to do in all rescues is to call loudly for help; continue to call for help until the rescue has been completed, or until help

---

## RESCUE FROM THE WATER

There are five problems to meet in making a rescue from the water:

Approaching the drowning person
Evading any dangerous "grips" made by the subject
Carrying the person through the water
"Landing" through shallow water or very deep water onto float or boat
Performing artificial respiration, if necessary

---

arrives. The second thing to do is to attempt the rescue without entering the water.

Often there is a boat, a line, a board, or some piece of floating material available, which can be pushed to the person in trouble, making the rescue more certain and less dangerous.

## APPROACHES AND CARRIES

*Rear Approach.* It is safest to approach a drowning person from the rear. Swim to a point directly behind the subject, reverse position of your

body, and reach one hand under her chin. Clutching the point of her chin in your palm, and bracing your forearm against her shoulder to control her head, you tilt her head backward as you kick vigorously, and stroke with your free arm to bring the subject to a level position. (Follow arm stroke through and push up small of back if necessary.) At first possible moment after leveling, go into a carry.

When it is impossible to approach from the rear, either the underwater or the surface approach can be used. The underwater approach is undesirable when the water is very muddy and it might be difficult to locate the subject under the water.

*Underwater Approach.* To make the underwater approach, swim to a point about six to ten feet in front of the subject, dive under to her foot level, and grasp her about the knee level, turning the subject about. Keep deep enough to avoid being clutched by the hands of the subject. During the surface dive and in reaching for the subject's knees, keep your arms straight before you, to avoid coming close enough to have her grasp you with her legs. After turning the subject, remain behind her and, without losing touch of her, come to the surface. As soon as your head is out, level her as in the rear approach.

*Surface Approach.* The surface approach is recommended only when the subject's eyes are underwater. To make a surface approach, swim toward the subject, facing her and reversing your position. Reach in with your right hand and grasp her right wrist, or with your left hand grasp her left wrist. Then use a powerful scissors kick and stroke, pulling subject toward you and turning her around. Clutching her chin with your free hand, level her, and proceed as in the rear approach.

*Head Carry.* Cover the subject's ears with the palms of your hands, thumbs toward her eyebrows, so that your middle fingers rest along her jawbone on both sides. Tilting her head backward, swim on your back, using frog or scissors kick. The rescuer should be in a half-sitting position, arms straight, head almost vertical, chin on chest, upper body about 45 degrees, and legs nearly parallel to the surface and about three feet below it. Rescuer must watch the subject's face at all times.

*Hair Carry.* From your position in back of subject, place your hand at the crown of her head, your fingers toward her forehead, grasping a handful of hair. With your hand in this position she will not roll over. Swim on your side with sidearm pull and scissors kick. Keep your holding arm straight.

*Cross-Chest Carry.* From a position in back of the subject, reach across her shoulder and chest, placing your hand under her farther armpit. (Shoulder blade is more comfortable if you can reach it.) Hold the subject so that your hip is directly under the center of her back and her shoulder is tight under your armpit. Swim on your side, using scissors kick and sidearm pull. In carrying the subject, keep her head out of the water and *hold her firmly in place with elbow against her chest.*

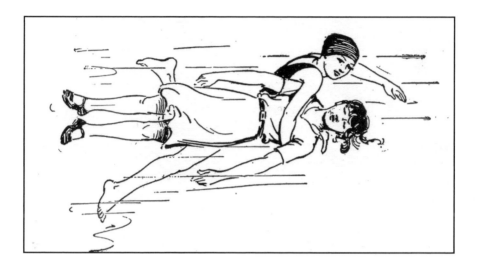

This carry is a favorite among lifesavers because the subject is completely under control.

*Tired Swimmer's Carry.* This carry is used only for a tired swimmer and not for a struggling, frightened one. It has a special surface approach of its own. The rescuer swims to the subject, telling her in a loud voice, "Put your hands on my shoulders," "Keep arms straight," "Lie on your back," "Spread your feet apart," "Watch my face," as she slowly swims breast stroke directly toward the subject, turning her in a half circle and heading her toward the landing. It is important to be able to "swim" the subject around quickly and efficiently. If the subject is tired, she wants to be picked up at once and not made to turn herself. The rescuer adapts the breast stroke arm pull and either frog or scissors kicks. Watch the subject's face while carrying.

## RELEASE METHODS

If the drowning person is struggling violently, so that it is impossible to subdue her or grasp her safely, it is a good idea to simply wait for her to exhaust herself before attempting to carry her to safety. Never attempt to strike the subject or to render her unconscious. Such a feat is almost impossible in the water. Breaking holds by inflicting pain is impractical, also. A desperate person fighting for her life will not be affected by such methods.

To avoid being caught in the grip of a drowning person, practice the proper approaches and use them in emergencies. The following release methods are effective, and it is advisable to be familiar with them, but the use of the proper approaches will lessen the danger of your being placed in such a position that release methods will be required.

Each of these methods is followed by the proper turn, getting the subject into a horizontal position, and starting the carry. In breaking holds, let yourself be submerged with the subject, performing the break underwater. This is done because a drowning person releases a hold more readily underwater, her constant desire being to climb to the surface to obtain air. Utilize this to escape. In leveling, the rescuer should be able to take a breath before the subject reaches the surface of the water.

*Front Strangle Hold.* You are grasped tightly around the neck from the front, the subject's head is over your shoulder. If the subject's head is over your right shoulder, put your right hand on her right cheek, little finger against the side of her nose, with thumb hooked under the angle of her lower jaw, and push her head toward your right. At the same time, put your left hand on the subject's, encircling her arm above the elbow and lift, following through—pushing toward the right. Then duck under the subject's arm as you raise it, pushing against her face and lifting her elbow until she is turned with her back to you. Continue to hold the elbow until you get your other hand back on the chin again to level the body, as in the rear approach.

If the subject's head is over your left shoulder, use your left hand on her left cheek, and your right hand to lift her left arm.

The efficiency of this method depends on the snap with which it is executed. Practice it slowly until you have the technique mastered, then perform the *push, lift,* and *duck,* all in one quick movement.

*Back Strangle Hold.* If you are grasped around the neck from the back, protect your throat with your chin. Grasp the subject's lower hand and *twist* it down and in toward her body, pushing up her elbow of the same arm with your free hand. Turn your face away and duck *under* this arm as you raise it, and continue twisting the subject's hand until she is turned back to you. Use your other hand for the chin pull, to get the subject's body flat on the surface, and swim with the hand that held her wrist. Shift to the cross-chest carry.

If the subject's left arm is the lower, use your left hand to raise her elbow and your right hand to twist her wrist. If her right arm is the lower, reverse the process.

*Double Grip on One Wrist.* The subject grasps your right wrist with both hands. Put your left hand, which is free, on the subject's left, with thumb on top and fingers under, ready to pull as soon as your foot is in position. The foot is used to push on the opposite shoulder as the arm is pulled toward you, retaining the hold on the wrist to level the subject by using the hand pull.

Use your left foot against the subject's right armpit, bringing it over her arms. Be careful not to kick her in the chest or breast. Be sure to push against the hollow of the shoulder and not below it. Straightening the leg as you pull with the left hand gives the necessary force to break the hold on your right wrist.

If you find that you are unable to reach the subject's shoulder with your foot, due to your shorter reach, bend your elbow until your foot is in contact.

When the hold is broken, turn her into position for a rear approach and carry. Should the left wrist be grasped, reverse the procedure, pulling with your right hand and pushing on the left shoulder with the right heel.

## ARTIFICIAL RESPIRATION

Some accidents—chiefly drowning, electric shock, and gas poisoning—cause the subject's breathing to stop. Suffocation, or asphyxia, with first unconsciousness and then death, occurs shortly after breathing ceases.

The first-aider can, however, carry on breathing for the subject by alternately compressing the chest and releasing the pressure, causing the air to flow out and in. This process is called artificial respiration and through its use many lives are saved.

*Caution.* Often inexperienced and excited persons attempt to administer artificial respiration when there is no need for such treatment. It is required only when the subject is unable to breathe. If the subject is brought from the water unconscious but still breathing, she requires treatment for shock or fainting. Send for a doctor at once, if there is anyone to send. If artificial respiration is needed when the subject has been brought safely to shore, waste no time in starting treatment.

The following is an approved method of artificial respiration.

Lay the patient face downward, one arm extended directly overhead, the other arm bent at elbow, with the face turned outward and resting on the hand and forearm, so that the nose and mouth are free for breathing.

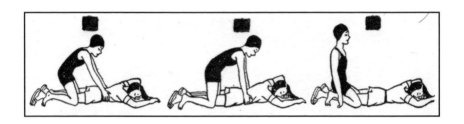

Kneel, straddling the patient's thighs. If the subject is a large person, straddle one leg only.

Place the palms of your hands on the small of her back with fingers resting on the ribs, the little fingers just touching the lowest ribs, with the thumbs and fingers in a natural position and the tips of the fingers just out of sight.

With arms held straight, swing forward slowly so that the weight of your body is gradually brought to bear upon the patient. Your shoulders should be directly over the heels of your hands at the end of the forward swing. Do not bend your elbows. This operation should take about two seconds.

Now immediately swing backward, so as to remove the pressure completely.

After two seconds, swing forward again. Repeat this double movement of compression deliberately twelve to fifteen times a minute and release, making a complete respiration in four or five seconds.

Continue artificial respiration without interruption until natural breathing is restored; if necessary, for four hours or longer, or until a physician declares the patient is dead.

As soon as this artificial respiration has been started, and while it is being continued, an assistant should loosen any tight clothing about the patient's neck, chest, or waist. *Keep the patient warm.* Do not give any liquids whatever by mouth until the patient is fully conscious. Do not allow her to stand or sit up.

Resuscitation should be carried on as close as possible to the place where the accident occurred. The patient should not be moved from this place until she is breathing normally of her own volition, and then moved only in a prone position. Should it be necessary to move the patient before she is breathing normally, resuscitation should be carried on during the time that she is being moved.

A brief return of natural respiration is not a certain indication for stopping the resuscitation. Not infrequently the patient, after a temporary recovery of respiration, stops breathing again. The patient must be watched, and if natural breathing stops, artificial respiration should be resumed at once.

It may be necessary to relieve the operator. This change should be made without losing the rhythm of respiration.

As soon as helpers arrive, put them to work. Send for a doctor, for blankets, and for hot tea or hot coffee for stimulant.

Organize your helpers while you are working. They will recognize you as a leader and gladly pitch in. All of this supplemental treatment is helpful but must not be allowed to interfere with, or interrupt for one second, the process of artificial respiration.

## RULES FOR SAFE SWIMMING

Do not swim with an upset stomach.

Do not enter the water until at least one hour has elapsed after eating.

Always swim with a buddy (a swimming partner).

Stay in your own swimming area (within a depth that is safe for you with your swimming ability).

Dive only in water of known depth.

Get out of the water when you get chilled or tired.

Do not swim after dark.

A long-distance swimmer ought to be accompanied by a boat manned by two expert swimmers.

## RAPPELLING

### FROM *BACK TO BASICS, THIRD EDITION*

One of the essential skills of rock climbers and mountaineers is rappelling—the technique of descending a cliff or steep slope by sliding down a rope. The skill can be of equal value to a backpacker. A hiker with a good rope and the knowledge of how to use it will often find the direct route down a cliff to be faster, easier, and a great deal more exhilarating than spending hours in the bush finding a way around. Caution: Rappelling must be mastered under the tutelage of an experienced climber before you attempt it on your own.

The principle of rappelling is to wrap the rope around the body in such a way that it supports the rappeller in an upright position, while its friction against her body allows her to control her rate of descent.

RAPPELLER FACES ANCHOR AND STRADDLES ROPE. RIGHT-HANDER WRAPS ROPE AROUND RIGHT HIP AND OVER LEFT SHOULDER.

RAPPELLER LEANS BACKWARD AGAINST ROPE, GRIPPING WITH LOWER, STRONGER HAND AS SHE STEPS BACK OVER THE EDGE

TO SLOW DESCENT, ROPE IS BROUGHT UP ACROSS THE SURFACE OF THE BACK; AT THE SAME TIME LOWER HAND SQUEEZES ROPE.

TO SPEED DESCENT, ROPE IS MOVED OUTWARD AND BEHIND WITH LOWER HAND, REDUCING FRICTION AGAINST BACK.

The rope must be long enough to hang double from the top of the cliff to the bottom, with plenty to spare to wrap around the body and loop around an anchor point on top. Only the best-quality climbing rope (minimum test strength 5,000 pounds) is used. The anchor must be totally secure and the rope should track around it easily so it can be retrieved from the bottom. Because the rope slides through the rappeller's hands and around her body as she descends, gloves and padding are important—it is not for nothing that the popular Dülfersitz technique is also known as the "hot-seat rappel."

## PADDLING A CANOE

The birch-bark canoe is the boat of many of the Native Americans, and our modern canoes are made, with some variations, on this model.

Many accidents happen in canoes—not because they are unsafe when properly handled but because they are unsafe when improperly handled—and many people do not take the trouble even to find out the proper way of managing a canoe. Many canoes have seats almost on a level with the gunwale, whereas, properly speaking, the only place to sit in a canoe is on the bottom; a seat raises the body too high above the center of gravity and makes the canoe unsteady and likely to tip over. It is, however, difficult to paddle while sitting in the bottom of a canoe, and the best position for paddling is that of kneeling. The size of the single-blade paddle should be in proportion to the size of the girl who uses it—long enough to reach from the ground to the tip of her nose. The bow paddle may be a little shorter.

You should learn to paddle equally well on either side of a canoe. When paddling on the left side the top of the paddle should be held by the right hand, and the left hand should be placed a few inches above the beginning of the blade. The old Indian stroke, which is the most approved modern method for all-round canoeing, whether racing or cruising, is made with the arms almost straight but not stiff—the arm at the top of the paddle bending only slightly at the elbow. This stroke is really a swing from the shoulder, in which there is little or no push or pull with the arm. When paddling on the left side of the canoe the right shoulder swings forward and the whole force of the body is used to push the blade of the paddle through the water, the left hand acting as a fulcrum. While the right shoulder is swung forward, the right hand is at the same time twisted at the wrist so that the thumb goes down; this motion of the wrist has the effect of turning the paddle around in the left hand—the left wrist being allowed to bead freely—so that, at the end of the stroke, the blade slides out of the water almost horizontally. If you should twist the paddle in the opposite direction it would force the head of the canoe around so that it would travel in a circle. At the recovery of the stroke the right shoulder swings back and the paddle is brought forward in a horizontal position, with the blade almost parallel to the water. It is swung forward until the paddle is at right angles across the canoe, then the blade is dipped edgewise with a slicing motion and a new stroke begins. In paddling on the right side of the canoe, the position of the two hands and the motion of the two shoulders are reversed.

Something should also be said about double paddles—that is, paddles with two blades, one at each end—as their use is becoming more general every year. With the double paddle a novice can handle a canoe head on to a stiff wind, a feat which requires skill and experience with a single blade. The doubles give greater safety and more speed and they develop chest, arm, and shoulder muscles not brought into play with a single blade. The double paddle is not to be recommended to the exclusion of the single blade, but there are many times when there is an advantage in its use.

In getting in or out of a canoe it is especially necessary to step in the very center of the boat; and be careful never to lean on any object— such as the edge of a wharf—outside of the boat, for this may capsize the canoe. In getting out, put down your paddle first, and then, grasping the gunwale firmly in each hand, rise by putting your weight equally on both sides of the canoe.

When it is necessary to cross the waves in rough water, always try to cross them "quartering," at an oblique angle. Crossing big waves at right angles is difficult and apt to strain a canoe, and getting lengthwise between the waves is dangerous.

In case of an upset the greatest mistake is to leave the boat. A capsized canoe will support any number of persons as long as they have strength to cling to it. A single woman or girl, in case of upsetting the canoe beyond swimming distance to land, should stretch herself flat upon the bottom of the canoe, with arms and legs spread down. She can thus lie in safety for hours till help arrives. When two persons are upset, they should range themselves one on each side of the over-turned boat;

and, with one hand grasping each other's wrists across the boat, use the other hand to cling to the keel or the gunwale. If the canoe should swamp, fill with water, and begin to sink, it should be turned over in the water. It is the air remaining under the inverted hull that gives the craft sufficient buoyancy to support weight.

Never overload a canoe. In one of ordinary size, about three persons should be the maximum number at any time, and remember never to change seats in a canoe when out of your depth.

## KAYAKING

### FROM *BACK TO BASICS, THIRD EDITION*

Kayaks are light, fast, and maneuverable; a beginner cannot just jump into one and paddle it off down the river. But once you master a few basic techniques under the eye of an experienced teacher, new

---

## BOATING AND CANOEING REGULATIONS

*COMMONLY USED IN GIRL SCOUT CAMPS*

1. Use boats and canoes only with the permission of the boating and canoeing counselor.
2. An experienced oarsman must be in every boat.
3. An experienced canoeist must be in every canoe.
4. Pass swimming test as required by camp before boating or canoeing.
5. Do not use boats or canoes during swimming periods.
6. Do not change seats or stand in boats or canoes.
7. Do not tow boats or canoes.
8. Stick to boat or canoe if it is capsized; it will hold you up (metal boats excepted).
9. Remember that a good boatsman or canoeist stays ashore in bad weather.
10. Discontinue the use of boats and canoes before dark.
11. At the end of a trip land the boat or canoe properly and return the oars or paddles to designated place.

worlds of boating will open up—from mountainous surf to roaring rapids—that would be off limits with any other kind of craft. And yet not all kayaking is so fast paced. Some two-place kayaks are designed for cruising and camping in flat water; and if your taste is for serenity, a kayak will serve just as well as a canoe in a tranquil pond or placid lake.

A kayak paddle has a blade at either end of its shaft. In use, one hand serves as a fulcrum while the other turns the paddle with a rotary motion. Paddles come in left- and right-hand models. The designation refers to the hand you prefer for rotation, not to whether you are a natural left-hander or right-hander. Quality in a paddle is vital; an inexpensive paddle is likely to break just when you need it most. Two- or three-piece paddles serve as well as spares carried beneath the deck or taped to it. Most kayakers prefer paddles with curved blades, since these furnish more thrust. Paddle size depends on your height. If you are six feet tall, the paddle length generally recommended is eighty-seven inches. For every two inches of height above or below six feet, add or subtract one inch of paddle.

If you are new to kayaking, practice a wet exit (getting out of a cap-sized kayak) before anything else—you will need the skill often. With someone standing by in waist-deep warm water, to offer help if you need it, take a deep breath and capsize the kayak. Unfasten the spray skirt by pulling the front loop, place both hands on the gunwales beside your hips, and push the boat away from you as you bend your hips to free your legs. Many beginners make the mistake of trying to get to the surface before they leave the boat. The secret is to get out of the boat first, then surface. Once you have the hang of it, practice the exit with your paddle. Do not let the paddle go, and do not lose contact with your kayak. Practice holding the paddle and the bow or stern grab-loop in one hand and swimming with the other.

Three more safety tips that can save your life: (1) Never go kayaking without a safety helmet and life jacket, (2) Make sure your kayak has been fitted with secure flotation bags, and (3) Always wear a wet suit in cold water.

## FIELD HOCKEY

### OBJECTIVE

Field hockey is a competitive game that is made up of two teams of eleven players on each side (this includes the goalie). The game only lasts for two halves, each of 30–35 minutes. So hurry up! The idea is to score more goals than your opponent.

### THINGS TO KNOW

### *THE FIELD…*

…should be at least a hundred yards long and sixty yards wide. This is separated by a line in the center and a twenty-five yard line on each side of the field. At each goal post there is a circle that marks the sixteen yards. It is within these sixteen yards in which the shot must be taken for it to count as a goal. The field is usually grass or artificial turf.

### *THE STICK…*

…usually made out of hardwood; has a curved head. On one side it is round and on the left hand side it is flat. You should always touch the ball with the flat side of the stick.

## *THE BALL...*

...is a bit larger than a baseball. It weighs approximately five and a half ounces and has a circumference of eight and thirteen sixteenths to nine and a quarter inches.

## *THE GOAL...*

...is the cage in which you need to put the ball in. They are usually seven feet high, twelve feet wide, and four feet deep.

## RULES

### *SCORE*

Goals can only be scored when the shot is taken within the circle that extends sixteen yards from the goal.

### *OVERTIME*

If you are playing in a competitive level and the score is tied after the game has concluded, you will go into overtime. This consists of two seven-and-a-half-minute periods. If you are playing at a high school competitive level, the game continues with two ten-minute periods. In both cases, overtime ends when one of the teams scores a goal. If the score is still tied by the end, then you would move on to penalty stroke competition.

### *PENALTIES*

Each team must pick five players that will alternate the penalty stroke against the opposing goalie.

### *FOULS, OFFENSES, & MISCONDUCT*

After you learn how to play, it is important to know the fouls (all those things you can't do)!

These include:

- Being mean; hitting or shoving an opponent.

– Obstructing the ball with any part of your body or stick or using your stick to resist an opponent.
– Hitting, hooking, holding, or interfering with an opponent's stick. When it comes to rough and dangerous play, the referee may warn the offending player with a green card, temporarily suspend with a yellow card, or permanently suspend with a red card.

## FREE HIT

This is awarded to the non-offending side after an infraction has occurred. These are usually done from the spot where the foul took place. No player of the opposing team may be within five yards of the ball when hit.

## PENALTY CORNER...

...is allowed when the following rules are broken:

– A breach of the rule by a defender within the circle that would have resulted in a free hit to the attacking team if the breach had occurred outside the circle.
– An intentional breach of the rule by the defenders outside the circle but within the twenty-five yard line.
– An intentional hit over the goal line by a defender from any part of the field. A penalty stroke is one-on-one, with the offensive player seven yards in front of the goal and the goalkeeper on the goal line, with all other players beyond the twenty-five yard line.
– A penalty stroke is awarded for any intentional breach by the defenders in the circle or for an unintentional breach by the defenders which prevents a sure goal.
– In a penalty corner, the ball is placed on the goal line at least ten yards from the nearest goal post. One attacking player hits the ball to a teammate just outside the striking circle line. A goal cannot be scored until the ball has traveled outside the circle. A shot on the goal may be attempted once the ball is played back into the circle. All attackers must be outside the circle before the hit is taken. On defense, a maximum of five defenders may be behind the goal line while the remaining defenders must be positioned beyond the center line.

– If the first shot at the goal is a hit (as opposed to a push, flick, or scoop), the ball must cross the goal line, at a height of no more than 460 mm (eighteen inches—the height of the backboard) before any deflection, for a goal to be scored.

### PENALTY STROKE

A penalty stroke is a one-on-one confrontation between an offensive player seven yards in front of the goal versus a goalkeeper on the goal line. All the other players must stand behind the twenty-five yard line. The goalkeeper stands with both feet on the goal line and does not move either foot until the ball is played. The offensive player can push or scoop the ball from the penalty spot. A penalty stroke is given for any intentional breach by the defenders in the circle or for an unintentional breach by the defenders should it prevent a sure goal.

### SIXTEEN-YARD HITS

When the attacking team plays the ball over the backline, the defense receives a sixteen-yard hit. The free hit is taken sixteen yards from the spot where the ball crossed the backline.

### THE PUSH-IN/HIT-IN

A push-in or hit-in is awarded to the opposition if a player hits the ball over the sideline. All other players and their sticks must be at least five yards away from the spot where the ball is put into play.

## SOCCER

Soccer is very likely the most popular game in the world; millions of people play it and billions of people watch it played every year. Soccer's World Cup is the most-watched sporting event of all time. Given this, it's not surprising that there's some dispute as to when and where soccer got its start. Many hold that the first recognizable soccer game was played in China over three thousand years ago. Others insist it began in Japan. Native Americans certainly played ball games that somewhat resembled our modern-day soccer.

---

## FREE KICKS, EITHER DIRECT OR INDIRECT, MAY BE AWARDED FOR THE FOLLOWING PENALTY FOULS:

- Holding an opponent
- Pushing an opponent
- Charging an opponent
- Tripping or attempting to trip an opponent
- Kicking or attempting to kick an opponent
- Striking or attempting to strike an opponent
- Handling the ball (except for a goalie in her own penalty area)
- Stopping the goalie from releasing the ball
- Delay of the game by a goalie

---

But the British—who sensibly enough call soccer "football"—were the ones who codified the rules and by 1800 had exported the game throughout their worldwide empire. By the 1930s there were soccer leagues on every continent.

### SIMPLE SOCCER

Ideally, each competing team or squad is composed of eleven players. There are, however, leagues and divisions in which there are six, eight, or ten players to a side. And really, you can have a good game with almost any number of players, so long as the sides are even.

The object, aim or—if you prefer—*goal* of soccer is to score points for one's side by putting the ball completely into your opponent's goal.

Dribbling is the skill, or art, of advancing and controlling the ball with your feet, but you may use any part of your body except your hands and arms to advance and control the ball. Except in the case of a throw-in, only the goalie may handle the ball with her hands, but only in her own penalty area.

When the ball goes out of bounds, play is restarted by a throw in, corner kick, or goal kick, depending which side last touched the ball and where exactly on the field the ball went out of play.

A penalty kick is awarded when a defender commits a foul inside her own penalty area. The kick is taken from the penalty spot. Except for the kicker and goalie, everyone else must be outside the penalty area, behind the ball, and at least ten yards from the penalty spot. After the initial kick, the kicker may not again touch the ball until another player touches it.

## BASKETBALL

In 1891, a fellow by the name of James Naismith nailed a peach basket to the wall of a gym and thereby invented the game we know as basketball. The game became widely and wildly popular and over the next several years, various refinements were made. A backboard was added, and the basket and backboard were positioned a good distance off the wall. This kept those early players from climbing the walls in order to score baskets. Amazingly, it took well over a decade for someone to figure out that if you cut the bottom out of the basket, allowing it to fall through, you won't have to retrieve the ball every time a basket is scored.

The following are Naismith's original thirteen rules for the game. Notice just how much appears to be borrowed from other popular field games, like soccer and volleyball:

*The object of the game is to put the ball into your opponent's goal. This may be done by throwing the ball from any part of the grounds, with one or two hands, under the following conditions and rules.*

1. *The ball may be thrown in any direction with one or both hands.*
2. *The ball may be batted in any direction with one or both hands.*
3. *A player cannot run with the ball. The player must throw it from the spot on which he catches it, or dribble the ball with one hand whilst running, allowances to be made for a man who catches the ball when running if he tries to stop.*
4. *The ball must be held by the hands. The arms or body must not be used for holding it.*

5. *No shouldering, holding, pushing, tripping, or striking in any way the person of an opponent shall be allowed; the first infringement of this rule by any player shall come as a foul, the second shall disqualify him until the next goal is made, or, if there was evident intent to injure the person, for the whole of the game, no substitute allowed.*

6. *A foul is striking the ball with the fist, violation of Rules 3, 4, and such as described in Rule 5.*

7. *If either side makes three consecutive fouls it shall count as a goal for the opponents (consecutive means without the opponents in the meantime making a foul).*

8. *A goal shall be made when the ball is thrown or batted from the grounds into the basket and stays there, providing those defending the goal do not touch or disturb the goal. If the ball rests on the edges, and the opponent moves the basket, it shall count as a goal. If the ball goes over the backboard and hits the side or the top of the backboard, then the ball is officially out of play.*

9. *When the ball goes out of bounds, it shall be thrown into the field of play by the person touching it. He has a right to hold it unmolested for five seconds. In case of a dispute the umpire shall throw it straight into the field. The thrower-in is allowed five seconds; if he holds it longer it shall go to the opponent. If any side persists in delaying the game the umpire shall call a foul on that side.*

10. *The umpire shall be the judge of the men and shall note the fouls and notify the referee when three consecutive fouls have been made. He shall have power to disqualify men according to Rule 5.*

11. *The referee shall be judge of the ball and shall decide when the ball is in play, in bounds, to which side it belongs, and shall keep the time. He shall decide when a goal has been made and keep account of the goals, with any other duties that are usually performed by a referee.*

12. *The time shall be two, fifteen minute halfs with a five minute break in between.*

13. *The side making the most goals in that time shall be declared the winner. In the case of a draw the game may, by agreement of the captains, be continued for five minutes after another jump ball.*

## CROSS-COUNTRY SKIING

### FROM *BACK TO BASICS, THIRD EDITION*

Cross-country skiing is a sport that takes you out into nature's wilderness at its loveliest and most unspoiled. It can be enjoyed even by novices, and, unlike downhill skiing, there are no long lift lines to contend with or expensive lift tickets to buy.

Dress warmly (in layers, so you can shed clothing as you warm up), and carry along a first aid kit, trail food, and a thermos of cocoa or other hot drink. Remember to treat cold weather with respect—do not go out alone and be sure to guard against frostbite, hypothermia, and snow blindness.

More than any other single topic the cross-country enthusiast talks, thinks, and worries about is wax. The right wax will give the ski good grip for a strong pushoff when the ski is standing still but allow the ski to glide almost without friction once it is sliding forward. A base wax is generally applied first, followed by a final, or kicker, wax. As a rule, the colder the temperature, the harder the wax should be. When the temperature is above freezing, a sticky liquid wax called klister is used.

An alternative to waxing, particularly appropriate for novice skiers, is the use of so-called waxless skis. These skis have special patterns on their running surfaces, such as diamond, fish scale, and stepped, or else have mohair strips embedded in their running surfaces.

Diagonal stride is the cross-country skier's basic step. First practice shuffling forward without poles. After you gain confidence, try "hopping" from one ski to the other as you transfer your weight. This hop, or kick as skiers call it, will provide enough thrust to let you glide forward on your other ski.

Full diagonal stride, shown sequentially, combines a kick with a simultaneous pole thrust on the opposite side. The movement is easy to learn because the arms and legs move as in

SKI TIP SHOULD REACH
WRIST. POLES SHOULD BE
SHOULDER HIGH.

natural walking. This skatelike stride, once mastered, has been said to give one the sensation of flying along the snow.

Snowplow and snowplow turn are downhill braking maneuvers particularly suitable for beginners or those carrying heavy packs. To do the snowplow, assume an exaggerated knock-kneed stance, and form the skis into a wedge with their inner edges digging into the snow. To make a snowplow turn, shift your weight to the ski on the side opposite the direction you want to turn—to the right ski for a left turn, to the left ski for a right turn. The arcs of snowplow turns are wide and sweeping. To slow down your descent, make the angle of the wedge wider; to speed it up, make the angle narrower.

## HORSE AND RIDER

*This is taken from a riding manual from the early 1900s.*

### THE SEAT

Our intention is not merely to teach people how to ride, but to reach that end quickly and safely. First, riding on horseback has, among its several aims, first the development of the human body along correct lines, and next the improvement of the rider's health. It is absolutely necessary that the learner apply herself to riding with the torso *normally erect*, yet *completely flexible.*

The first of them is this: When carried thus, the rider's torso becomes *automatically* placed *as close to the saddle as possible*, and this *is absolutely necessary for her safety.* This therefore enables her to learn to feel what her

mount is *going to do*, and she can thus thwart that motion, if it happens to be an undesirable one, such as bucking.

One of the great advantages that result from having the seat automatically as close as possible to the saddle arises from the fact that no effort other than the *natural carriage of the torso* is necessary to maintain it there.

Consequently, no constant tightening of the knees being necessary to achieve closeness of contact with the saddle, the rider who follows this method does *not* have to continually strain her legs in trying to get the famous "grip" on the horse that so many people advocate. While the *whole* interior side of the thighs and of the knees *must* be kept *constantly adherent to the saddle*, from the instant one gets on the animal's back, to the moment one dismounts, this closeness of contact *must be effortless*, a result which is obtained by the mere keeping, *at all times and under all circumstances, the heels on a level lower than the toes.*

When, in consequence of certain undesired motions of the horse, greater assurance to "stick" on to him becomes necessary, it can be obtained by an increased forcing of the lower legs downward, and therefore by the increased lowering of the heels, which *automatically* also results in the tightening not merely of the knees but of the whole of the thighs *downward*, from the seat to just below the knees.

As soon as the torso, or any other part of the body, loses its flexibility, it proportionately and automatically increases its weight; and while the increase in the weight of the legs is advisable in many circumstances, the increase in the weight of the torso is *inadvisable always*, because it renders the rider top-heavy. Besides, that flexibility of the torso enables the rider automatically to follow the motions of the horse; and as that suppleness means also "diminution of weight," it enables her to feel much less the "bumps" consequential to her mount's ordinary motions, as for example at the trot, or when, sometimes in sheer joy, she gives a little bound or two.

One of the conditions necessary to maintain the torso erect is for the elbows to be kept, at all times, in close contact with the hips. But, while this contact must be "close" it must not be "forced," and therefore it must be brought about merely by the normal perpendicularity of the arms. As this elbow-posture should be present even when the hands, and the forearms, have to be used with prompt motions, as for example to stop one's mount quickly, it is *absolutely necessary* for the beginner to learn to *shorten the reins* correctly—as explained further on—as soon as her torso has been properly placed on the saddle. If she is not taught this manipulation of the reins without delay, she will inevitably contract the habit of pulling on the animal's mouth without even thinking of shortening the reins and, her elbows having to be displaced for this purpose, they will poke either backwards, or sideways, or both.

Thus, not only will her arms be stiffened but her back also, and the combination of those untoward motions of hands, arms, and back will displace her seat and prejudice her firmness in the saddle.

Since one of the requisites for the rider to acquire proper balance is that the balancing parts—the legs—be well placed, it is necessary that her stirrups be sufficiently *long* to allow for her getting as far down into her saddle as she possibly can, yet sufficiently *short* to have a slight bend, and to enable her to carry the heels *constantly* at a level lower than the toes.

The bend at the knees must be "slight," *especially with beginners*, (1) so that they do not accustom themselves to "depend on their stirrups" for security, as those appendages should come to be considered as mere ornaments when beginners have advanced to the stage of being good riders; (2) the stirrups should be of the length shown in above so that the rider's legs are not cramped; and (3) they should be of a length for the rider's seat not to be thrust on the hind part of the saddle, called the cantle, as it inevitably is when the stirrups are too short.

## THE HANDS

The rider's hands must be carried at a normal height, therefore *at the level of her elbows*, where they can easily be lifted or lowered, *separately or conjointly* as conditions presented by the animal's conformation or by her motions may require, or as conditions of guidance and control may necessitate.

They must be carried close, though not sticking, to each other and *relaxedly rounded* with the thumbs over each relative forefinger; the nails of the other fingers and the first knuckles facing the rider; the second knuckles facing each other. With the hands carried thus, the thumbs and forefingers will be automatically holding the reins firmly, while the other fingers will be able to open and close on the reins as may be necessary, according to the animal's response to the actions of the rider's hands and legs, without running the risk of reins slipping out of them.

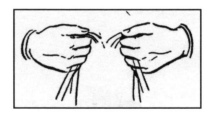

The ordinary actions that have to be made by the hands must be effected *from the wrists*. There are extraordinary conditions that require the hands to be used in different ways. But the person desirous of riding properly, and of acquiring the priceless quality of *good hands*, must apply herself *from the start of her equestrian career* to using the hands *from the wrists*. In order to do this properly she must turn the palms of her hands *upwards* when tensing the reins, which is called "taking," and return them a little further than in their original position when she releases the tension on the reins, called "giving."

If the rider follows faithfully all the foregoing advice, she will find herself ready to ride properly, comfortably, securely, and elegantly, conditions which are fundamental for the equestrian exercise.

## STIRRUPS AND SADDLE

The best way to adjust a rider's stirrup, when she is on horseback, is to have her sit erect, in the center of the saddle with legs hanging at full length along the sides of the horse, and allow the stirrup-plate to reach just below the anklebone. Later on, this stirrup length might prove slightly too long for practical purposes; but a stirrup longer than *practically* advisable—that is, one reaching just below the anklebone—should be given to her during her first lessons, in order that she learn *not* to depend on them for support and thus that she acquires *balance*.

When the stirrups are measured, the rider has simply to lift her toes to be able to slip her feet in the stirrups, which she should immediately

begin learning to do *without looking down at them*. She will find that this automatically gives her knees the correct bend, and she will therefore have the correct leg posture.

Bad habits being easy to acquire but difficult to eradicate, especially in horsemanship, it is absolutely necessary for the learner to accustom herself *not to look down at her stirrups* while they are being slipped on to her feet, as she will thus eventually acquire the exceedingly useful knack of being able to slip them on and off at will, and at all gaits, as will be explained later on. When in the saddle, the rider must remind herself to keep her seat *as low down as possible* in the saddle, at all times.

She will do this more easily by trying from time to time to "feel" the saddle with the end of her spinal cord.

The torso of the rider must be in the center of the saddle, not only when looked at from the side but also when looked at from behind, because one of the principal conditions for her acquiring balance, and incidentally for the horse's being "in balance," is that *the line of the rider's spine be at all times exactly in line with her mount's spine*. Sitting thus in the center of the saddle she will have the further advantage of leaving fully two or three finger-widths of saddle-space free behind her, which will protect the end of her spine from being hurt by the end of the saddle.

The best-made saddle for all purposes is the Saumur-saddle, because it has a "dip" which suits conveniently the form of the base of the torso. This is important, because in order for her to govern her mount

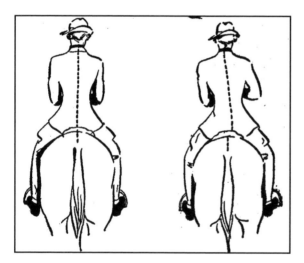

properly and easily the rider's lower legs must *not* be thrust forward but must be carried when "at rest" in such a position that a perpendicular may be drawn from his nose to the tips of his toes.

Thus her lower legs will cover the line of her mount's girths, and to make sure of her legs being properly placed she will require only *to see her toes without having to bend the head forward*. The position "at rest" does not imply the horse's immobility but simply means that the rider's legs are not being used for the purpose of guiding or controlling her mount. Thus it is that she may be at full gallop, yet holding her legs in the position "at rest."

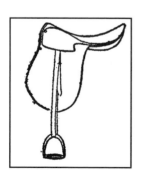

# HISTORY AND CONFORMATION
# OF THE HORSE

*By Ivy Maddison*

## EQUIPMENT

Bridle: This is the headgear. This includes the reins and bit.

Bit: This is a piece made of steel that is placed in the horse's mouth.

Reins: This is a leather strap that is attached to the horse's bit of head piece that come out on either side. These are used to control and direct the horse. You can control the horse to stop, slow down, turn left, right, or backward, by using the reins.

Halter: This is what is placed on the horse's head to lead or tie.

Saddle: This is the "seat" that is placed over the back of the horse.

Stirrup: There are two stirrups that hang from a leather strap on each side of the saddle. It consists of two rings with a flat bottom in which the rider places her feet.

The history of the horse has been well covered by other writers but since it is a subject which always interests horsewomen, I shall give a few of the main facts for the benefit of readers who may not have met them elsewhere.

The native country of the horse cannot with certainty be traced but we are told that in 1740 BC, she was domesticated by the Egyptians and in 1500 BC, she constituted the principal strength of their army. We hear of the horse in Greece as early as 1450 BC, when the Olympic games included chariot and horse races. Through ancient records we trace her next to Arabia and Persia from where she gradually found her way to other parts of the world.

One of the first and most important breeds was the Barb, named from its native Barbary, and also found in Morocco, Fez, and the interior of Tripoli. Although noted for her fine and graceful action, this horse had not the spirit, speed, or endurance of the Arab. The Barb was not so high as the latter, her chest round and the joints inclined to be long. Her head was particularly beautiful. The Barb was early introduced into

England and the famous horse of that breed, "The Godolphin Arabian" as she was called, was the origin of some of the best racing blood which we have today.

The Arabian horse did not reach the standards which we now associate with her until the thirteenth century. Like the Barb she has always been noted for her beautiful head. A square forehead, an eye both prominent and brilliant, small, well-shaped ears, a light body and narrow chest, sloping shoulders and high withers, are other characteristics of this breed which has ever excelled in disposition, speed, and courage.

One historian declares that there was a horse in a certain section of Central Africa which was superior to either the Arab or the Barb and possessed the best qualities of both breeds. Horses found in other parts of Africa, however, were usually weak and intractable.

The earliest record of the horse in Great Britain is contained in Julius Cæsar's history of his invasion of that Island, in which he says that the British army was accompanied by numerous war chariots drawn by horses which the enemy handled with great dexterity. He himself was so impressed with them that he took many back to Rome. It was probably at this time that the British equine got its first cross.

About AD 930, King Athelstane, who appears to have interested himself in the breed, made a law that no horse should be exported from England. In a document dated 1000 AD, we have a statement of the relative cost of the horse which was thirty shillings, while an ass was valued at twelve, a cow at twenty-four pence, and a pig at eighteen pence. An improvement of the equine began in the reign of Henry I and the first Arabian horse was introduced when Henry II was king. As more foreign blood was imported the English became very jealous of these animals and heavy penalties for exporting them were imposed.

Henry VIII fixed a standard below which no horse should be kept. The lowest heights were fifteen hands for a stallion and thirteen for a mare. Magistrates were ordered to destroy all horses under the standard heights as well as those animals which they considered unlikely to produce a valuable breed. Moreover, all gentry and farmers were compelled to keep and raise horses.

About this time there was a book written by A. Fitz-Herbert, judge of Common Pleas, entitled *Book of Husbandry* which quotes the qualities of a good horse. She is supposed to have fifty-four properties,—two of a man, two of a badger, four of a lion, nine of an ox, nine of a hare, nine of a fox, nine of an ass, and ten of a woman. I do not know what all these points were but the following quotation is often given:

"A horse should have three qualities of a woman,—broad chest, round hips, and long mane.

"Three of a lion,—countenance, courage, and fire.

"Three of an ox,—eye, nostrils, and joints.

"Three of a sheep,—nose, gentleness, and patience.

"Three of a mule,—strength, constancy, and foot.

"Three of a deer,—head, legs, and short hair.

"Three of a wolf,—throat, neck, and hearing.

"Three of a fox,—ear, tail, and trot.

"Three of a serpent,—memory, sight, turning.

"Three of a cat,—running, walking, and suppleness."

It is generally believed that there were no horses in North America before the coming of the Spaniards. Cabera-de-Vaca brought some to this country in 1527. The descendants of these animals are the mustangs. The first thoroughbred was imported to Virginia from England in 1730 and this state, and Kentucky, became the home of the thoroughbred horse in our country. This strain is the foundation of every riding and driving horse in America.

So through the interest and careful breeding of past centuries, the present horse has at last been developed. Curiously enough she is a subject concerning which many people pride themselves on being well posted who in reality are quite ignorant. We must remember that every steed has something good and something bad about her and that a knowledge of good conformation will enable us to determine whether her good points outnumber those that are inferior.

A good looking horse is not necessarily one that is well made, as an animal's head, neck, and shoulders are the points which we are apt to notice first. On the other hand, when we pick to pieces some ewe-necked, ugly headed, angular steed, we may find that she has fairly good conformation. In speaking of the latter we mean a horse with a long front, a fairly high wither, flat, sloping shoulders, a short back, big girth, strong quarters, and beyond all, good bone and properly put on legs. An animal's head and neck, although they denote the breeding so essential for show purposes and hunting, do not affect her work-

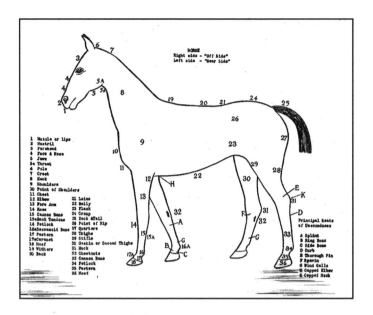

ing capacities as much as some other characteristics. They do, however, sometimes influence her gaits.

In order to give you a good ride, a horse must be light in hand. For this purpose her neck should be thin and well cut under the jaw, and her head small to better enable her to flex the former. The crest should be firm and arched rather than concave. A wide jaw, broad forehead, and straight nose are other desirable points. An animal with a Roman nose, known in England and Ireland as a nappy horse, is apt to be too fond of her own way, and those with concave faces are generally wanting in intelligence.

The expression of the eyes and ears give indication of an animal's character. Small, pig eyes and long, lop ears denote a sulky disposition. The eye should be full, bright, and prominent. Small eyes which show the whites are often a sign of bad temper. The ears ought to be of moderate size and tapering, the nostrils large and easily dilated, the muzzle small, and the lips firm and fine.

We come now to those points which contribute directly to the four most essential characteristics of a horse: strength, speed, endurance, and quality. She should have flat bone and substance, though only carrying a little weight. The shoulder should slope well back to the withers and be muscled up, yet without superfluous fat.

A shoulder is often deceiving from the ground, however, for a horse with straight shoulders will sometimes be able to use them freely. In fact most harness horses with a great deal of action are inclined to be straight as the shoulder muscles lift the front legs and when the former are upright, there is a more direct line for the muscles to pull. Such a horse however cannot take as long a stride with ease as the horse with the sloping shoulder. Also her gallop is affected for her efforts are directed in picking up her feet instead of throwing them out. The oblique shoulder is therefore preferable for the hack or hunter because both animals should move freely. The latter must of course be well able to gallop. Nevertheless, some animals with sloping shoulders are tied up, so that in order to determine how well they use them, it is always advisable to get on their backs.

The withers should be fairly high, thin, and run well back as this offers a larger space for the shoulder muscles to expand, and the saddle will then be on the center of gravity. If the wither does not run back, the saddle will be too far forward, thereby shortening the animal's front. Moreover, on a low withered or "mutton" shouldered horse there is nothing to keep the saddle steady and a rider is forced to depend entirely on her girths.

The back should be short and straight, but in proportion to the rest of the body. A sway-backed horse is usually weak and unable to carry much weight. In many instances this defect comes from old age or hard work. The girth ought to be deep and the ribs well sprung. A flat sided animal seldom has stamina. The last rib should come within a span of the hip bone. A horse must be muscular over his loins, particularly for weight carrying purposes and jumping.

The quarters depend largely on the condition of an animal. When she is fat they should look fairly round and appear broad when one stands behind her as this denotes strength. Animals with narrow quarters often have speed but they are poor weight carriers. The thighs must be well developed and deep. The second thighs should also be long and muscular.

The rump should be slightly arched, the tail set on high and carried well away from the body when the horse is in motion. A tail that is set on low lessens the smart appearance of an animal and is particularly undesirable with a saddle horse who must look "flashy."

Every horse should have flat bone, clean limbs, and front legs that are set well under her. The forearms must be muscular. Looking at the knee in profile the cannon bone and radius (the upper and lower bones of the foreleg) are nearly in a straight line. Some horses are calf kneed which in my opinion is a serious fault because the back tendons and ligaments are then more liable to sprain as the pasterns of such an animal are usually inclined to be upright. This gives the tendons the whole force of the concussion. If, on the other hand, the pasterns are sloping and strong, they act as a shock absorber for the leg and foot. There is the opposite formation of being over at the knees which is generally the result of hard work or old age. However, if this fault is slight, it will seldom affect a horse except for show purposes. I have known several really good hunters whose way of going and style of fencing were not hampered by this defect.

When a horse stands at ease her hind legs should be well under her. The hocks must be large and flat. A good ride depends greatly on hock action for if an animal drags her hocks the rider must do most of the work. Since a horse jumps off her hocks they are also an important point in a hunter.

The feet of a well-bred horse should be strong and of fair size. Little, contracted feet often cause him to go sore with work. The outside of the hoof must be smooth as rings and ridges are frequently the sign of disease or injury. The frog ought to be well-formed and of the consistency of hard rubber so that it will not easily bruise. The sole of the foot should also be in good condition. With a bad foot bruise recovery is usually slow and the injury may result in navicular or some other foot disease. The heel should be broad and never allowed to contract for this is another cause of lameness.

A horse's age is, of course, an important question for the prospective buyer. The diagram may prove useful to the reader in determining this point.

We come now to the principal points of unsoundness, a knowledge of which would save many a purchaser the money she has invested in an unserviceable horse. I may also add here that ignorance on this subject has frequently prevented riders from buying an animal admirably well-suited to their needs because the mention of some bump or scar has frightened them, causing them to turn around and purchase a second horse whose defect is less easily detected but more serious. For just as practically no animal approaches perfection in conformation, so very few are without some slight blemish. The following list includes the main points of unsoundness.

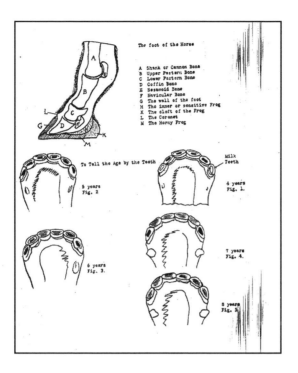

## CURB

A curb is a thickening of the ligaments and other tissues of the back part of the hock just below the hock joint and is due to rupture or sprain. It is usually quite prominent giving a curved line instead of the normally straight appearance when the hock is viewed from the side. The sprain generally causes lameness which, however, will likely disappear with rest. The enlargement stays but can often be reduced by blistering. A horse with a curb is always unsound because hard work will usually make him lame.

## BONE SPAVIN

An inflammation of some of the bones forming the hock joint is called a bone spavin. It is detected by an enlargement, or bunch, on the inside of the joint, slightly to the front. Some spavins come higher than others and the high ones are the most serious as they interfere more with the movement of the joint. There is lameness in the first stages but after this a horse is usually fit for slow work. When leaving the stable they will often show a stiffness which they work out after a mile or two.

## CAPPED HOCK

A capped hock is an enlargement on the point of the hock which is usually caused by blows or kicks. Horses that kick badly in the stable often have capped hocks from hitting them on the side of the stall. This defect, although hard to get rid of, seldom makes an animal lame.

## SPLINT

An enlargement on the side of the fore leg below the knee and between the splint bone and the cannon bone is known as a splint. Occasionally splints also appear on the outside of the leg and on the hind leg. A high splint is the most dangerous as it is more likely to affect the articulation of the knee joints and cause ulceration. Also, a splint that is toward the back of the leg is more serious as it is then apt to interfere with the back tendons. One that is well-forward and in the middle of the cannon bone, however, will seldom give any trouble after it has developed. A splint can cause lameness. When it hardens and becomes fully developed the irritation stops and usually the lameness with it. Personally, I consider splints one of the least serious of the defects which I am mentioning here.

## RING BONE

A ring bone comes on any of the four legs on the pastern joint just above the hoof—rarely on the coffin joint. There is inflammation of the joint followed by the welding together of the large and small pastern bones. In many cases where there is no ring of bone around the joint, a bony bunch appears at one or both sides. Other times, a complete ring can be seen around the front of the joint. In the first stages of this trouble lameness is present which, like a spavin, improves when fully developed. A horse with ring bone, however, will stand very little work.

## SIDE BONE

This comes on either side of the foot at the top of the hoof and close to the heel where there are lateral cartilages which allow the fatty frog and soft tissues of the heel to expand as the horse brings her weight on her foot. When this cartilage turns to bone it may cause lameness for a hack or hunter. The only cure is to have it removed by a surgical operation. This form of unsoundness is seldom found on any but heavy truck horses.

## WIND PUFFS

Wind puffs, which are sacks of joint oil, form puffy tumors which appear on either side of the leg above the fetlock joint between the back tendons and the bone. Wind puffs, or wind galls, practically never affect a horse's soundness but they are a blemish as well as being a sign of wear, for they generally appear on animals who have been worked hard.

*Thorough Pin*—A puffy enlargement much like a wind puff occurring halfway between the point of the hock and the front of the back joint. This comes both on the inside and outside of the leg and is more common with draft horses. A thorough pin seldom causes lameness.

## BOWED TENDON

A bowed tendon comes from a strain of the back tendons. If slight, the condition will be relieved by the application of cold water bandages. However, if the animal breaks down and the tendons swell greatly, recovery is apt to be very slow and with fast work or jumping the horse will be liable to sprain again. Such a horse is often suitable for road riding.

*Capped Elbow* or *Shoe Boil*—Situated on the elbow and first appears as a soft fleshy bag containing a small amount of watery fluid. This often results in a bad boil or infected sore and is due to a horse bruising her elbow with her shoe when lying down.

## STRINGHALT

A nervous affection in which the muscles of the hind leg are excessively flexed so that the hind foot is jerked up toward the stomach. This defect is only noticeable when the horse is moving.

## BROKEN-WINDED

Broken-winded horses are those which make a noise and, although unsound, are quite capable of doing ordinary work. In fact, abroad they often hunt animals which make a noise.

One frequently finds what is called a rough-winded horse—an animal which, though she can be heard quite plainly, does not seem to have her galloping ability impaired. Again, we find one who is only a slight whistler and yet cannot gallop two miles. When a horse is soft and out of condition she will often blow, causing the novice to think her broken-winded. While the latter is quite a different noise, it is always wise to have a veterinarian examine the animal when there is any doubt, for only experience will enable one to detect whether or not a horse is unsound in this respect.

## HORSE SENSE

*By Count de Souza*

*(Count di Souza's manner of expressing himself seems quaint today, but he was a master horseman and teacher.)*

There are so few nowadays who know how to hold a horse properly for another person to mount, that I consider it necessary to say how it should be done. Standing on the animal's near (right) side, at approximately the level of her girths, one should pass the right hand *under* the curb-reins and take the snaffle-reins with that hand *upside down*, the index finger between those reins; the other three fingers around the left snaffle-rein and the thumb helping the index finger hold them.

While doing this with the *right* hand, she must hold the stirrup leather as close to the stirrup as possible with the *left* hand, and weigh on it with sufficient strength to prevent the saddle from being displaced on the animal's back by the rider's weight bearing on its left stirrup at the moment of mounting.

She should stand with the feet slightly apart in order to have a good purchase in case the horse were to move, and in order to prevent this

she should be prepared to check the horse *gently* by means of the reins and also by some calming words, if necessary. Some people, desiring to prevent the horse from moving, pull on the horse before the animal does move, an action which works negatively as, nine times out of ten, it actually causes her to move, whereas she probably would not have had the slightest idea of doing so if she had been held by a calm, quiet hand.

When starting on a ride, walk your horse first for some little time, so that she gets her bearings, as it were; and during a ride do not cause her to move at only one gait all the time, even if it be the walk, for it is as tiring for a horse to walk only, as it is for a woman to walk slowly—try it. Therefore intersperse the ride with walk, slow trot—unless the weather be cold—walk again, a right canter, walk again, another trot—more or less faster than the first—another walk, a left canter, another walk, another trot, perhaps still faster than the others; and return to the stable *always at a walk*, for the last block or so of distance, unless there be some *good* reason to reach the shelter without delay. Try always to quiet the horse after having turned her stable-ward, whatever the gaits one chooses to follow as allowing animals to get excited when turned towards home is one of the surest means for making runaways of them.

Always ride a horse with a view to improving her, even if she be a rented livery stable animal, as in the first place you will improve your riding while improving her, because the improvement of the one cannot take place without the other.

Watch the animal's breathing, especially if she seems to be slowing down on her own accord. It is cruel to overwork a horse, just as it is inhumane to overwork a woman. It is always a proof of unladylikeness to bring a horse back to her stable sweaty and panting.

Do not allow a horse to drink on returning from a ride but let her stand about an hour before watering her, if she has worked slightly hard. If not, half an hour will be sufficient.

Similarly, do not give her oats on her return from a ride but allow her to eat hay, straw, or grass. Oats should be given a horse after she has rested and drunk. Do not ride her immediately on her having finished eating oats, but give her *at least* half an hour's time for her digestion to be well under way. If, on your ride, you meet a clear pond or stream you can allow your mount to drink, *provided* you intend to move her a little briskly immediately after. Even so, do not allow her to take a long drink, but "cut" it twice or thrice by picking up the reins and lifting the animal's head from the water during a minute or so between drinks.

If the horse you are riding puts her ears back and makes the slightest sign of wishing to bite the horse next to her—or even the one ahead of her—prevent her from doing so by shaking the reins, or even yanking them *if necessary*. Call her attention away by scolding her, as even the mere motion of the ears backwards is a sign that the animal has a biting or kicking tendency and is on the point of doing one or the other or both.

If the horse you are riding kicks, put the shoulders quickly backwards, in order to be as firmly seated in the saddle as possible, and increase this firmness by shoving the heels as low as possible. But do not lean the shoulders too far forward; you may be thrown and at the same time lift the animal's head so as to prevent her from kicking again and simultaneously attack her *vigorously* with both legs, twice or thrice consecutively, as much for punishment as for maintaining the movement forward, which she has to suspend in order to kick. Yet this movement forward must not result in *excitement*, as some professional kickers will "fire out" even when moving fast.

Do not allow your mount to break from the trot to the canter, especially not to do so *at her will*, for if you allow her to do so you teach her not to have a good fast trot, which is very agreeable for both the horse and her rider, *if not abused*.

When riding in company the speed of the horses should be regulated on the speed of the slowest horse, or on the ability of the poorest rider; for it is quite as impolite for a rider to move ahead of another under the circumstances as it would be rude for a person to move away without notice from a person with whom she was walking. Furthermore, in riding there is the danger of a horse becoming obstreperous when suddenly left alone and thus running the chance of throwing her rider, especially if that person is a beginner.

When passing another rider on a road, do not go too close to her, as her mount *might* be a kicker and might "fire one" at your horse and incidentally at you.

Do not stand at striking distance from a horse that is being girthed, as at that moment all horses, even the gentlest, snap the teeth and bite, even if not biters, and any one of them is therefore apt to hurt you.

If your mount shies at something do not clutch at the reins nervously nor "beat her up" for it, as that would only make matters worse. Therefore, calm her down while *forcing her to pass it*, but you might not *insist* on her going *very* near it, unless you were a good rider; yet do not let her *rush away* past it because that will induce her to believe that danger *really lurks there*, since her rider has allowed her to move away from it quickly.

Do not treat your horse as if she were a piece of machinery but consider her as the sentient being *that she is*, since she is endowed with several of the feelings humans have—and possibly more than we know. Science may yet discover that she is endowed with some other feelings than the few with which we credit her.

That being so, punish her as she may *deserve, not* according to your caprice, and only to the extent and in the manner she deserves, suspending all punishment *instantly* when she stops doing wrong. Do not punish her *angrily*, as the horse feels her rider's anger—even when she is not being punished. Moreover, reward her by *gentle caresses* (*not* the near-blows some people advise) also *only when she deserves them* but not as bribes to coax her into doing things. Speak to her encouragingly, approvingly, scoldingly, or lovingly, as she may *deserve*. But, just as you must not abuse with punishment, you must not abuse with reward because the horse accustomed to receiving it without reason will cease appreciating it when she does deserve it, and its results will therefore be unsatisfactory.

Although you may never have to use a riding whip, it is

very advisable for you to learn to carry a crop and to learn to carry it as easily in one hand as in the other.

Always wear gloves while riding, as the continued friction of the reins may cause chafings which are unpleasant and may easily become infected, the reins being abundantly covered with germs, however clean they may be kept. The best gloves for riding purposes are the suède and they must be large enough to fit loosely.

When riding always think: "Were I a horse would I like to be treated thus?" Yet—don't let your mount *do*, or *go*, as she pleases, for *she must obey you.*

## ABOUT DRESSAGE

*By Emma Keast Banasiak, aged 13*

In French the word *dressage* means training. Dressage is a series of movements in which the horse and rider move as one. It originated in ancient times when it was used in battle. Many of the commands the French used in battle then are used in competitions now. Nowadays, people compete in dressage competitions all over the world.

The gold standard for modern dressage is Parelli. In Parelli exercises you perform a dressage test without a bridle; sometimes a person will put a piece of twine around the neck of her horse but that's about it. In Parelli you are only allowed your "natural" aids (legs), you are not allowed to use "artificial" aids (whip, spurs, or a standing/running martingale). Parelli exercises are named after Pat Parelli. Parelli rode without tack (saddle, bridle, running/standing martingale) or any "artificial" aids.

Another amazing form of Dressage is practiced with the famous Spanish Lipizzaner. These horses are highly trained and are some of the best in the world. To train one of these horses you ride special, pure bred Lipizzaners and use equipment made specially for this discipline.

In Dressage you memorize and practice for a test consisting of various movements. Some common movements and terms are:

*Flying Change*—When a rider changes leads without breaking the canter.

*Extended, Collected, Working, Medium*—These are different variations of the trot and canter.

*Piaffe*—A movement in which it looks like a horse is trotting in place.

*Serpentine*—This movement consists of either two or three loops in which you almost zig zag around the arena.

## BADMINTON

(Court Dimensions: 44 feet x 22 feet (double)/44 feet x 17 feet (single) Net Height: 5 feet, one inch on the sides/5 feet on the center of court)

### THE OBJECTIVE

Actually there are two objectives in badminton. The first is to hit the shuttlecock, also known as shuttle or birdie, back and forth over a net without allowing it to hit the floor on your side of the net. The second is to hit the shuttle to the opponent's side of the court in a way that she is unable to return it. This is done by using various strokes such as net shot and smashes.

This game can be played in singles or in doubles.

### A FEW BASIC RULES

1. A coin toss determines who will serve first.
2. The player may not touch the net with the racket.
3. The birdie may not come to rest or be carried on the racket.
4. If the birdie hits the net on its way across during play it can continue.
5. The player cannot reach over the net to hit the birdie.
6. The racket must make contact with the birdie below the waist on a serve.
7. The server and receiver must stand within their courts until the serve is made.

### LETS

"Let" refers to bringing a play to a stop. For example, if there is an unforeseen or accidental occurrence such as:

- The birdie is caught in the net (except on service).
- During service, the receiver and server commit a fault at the same time.

- The server serves before the receiver is ready.
- During play, the birdie disintegrates and the base separates from the rest of the shuttle.

## THE BIRDIE IS NOT IN PLAY WHEN

- It gets caught in the net.
- It strikes the net or post and falls on the striker's side of the court.
- It hits the surface of the court or a "fault" or "let" has occurred.

## SCORING

The score consist of the best of three games. In doubles and men's singles, the first side to score fifteen points wins the game. In women's singles, the first side to score eleven points wins the game.

If the score becomes ten-all in women's singles, the side which first scores ten can choose to continue the game to eleven points or to "set" the game at thirteen points.

The side that wins the game serves first in the next game. Only the serving side can add a point to its score.

## FAULTS OCCUR WHEN

- The birdie lands outside the court boundaries, passes through or under the net, does not pass the net, touches the ceiling or side walls, or touches the person or any other object.
- The initial point of contact with the birdie is not on the striker's side of the net. (The striker may, however, follow the shuttle over the net with the racket in the course of a stroke.)
- A player touches the net or invades the opponent's court.
- A player invades an opponent's court so that she is so obstructed or distracted that it does not allow the other player from making a hit.
- A player distracts an opponent by shouting or making gestures.
- The birdie is caught and held on the racket and then hit during a stroke.
- The birdie is hit twice by the same player with two strokes.

# NATURE

## HIKING/WHY BOTHER?

Irresistible days occur at almost any season of the year, when a desire wakes in every girl's heart to go adventuring over the hills, to feel the soft turf underfoot, to smell the fragrant wood fire, and to get into friendly touch with nature's enchantments.

In answer to this call An Adventurous Girl goes tramping away from paved roads and the hum of motors to meet the joys and mysteries of the out of doors with a gypsy spirit. She knows the rhythmic swing that puts the miles lightly behind her, the glory of the unfolding panorama, and the tantalizing beckoning of the horizon. She enjoys facing wind and weather and cooking over open fires.

Hiking is a good old Cornish word and means walking with good will. Emerson defined walking as follows:

"Walking is a fine art; there are degrees of proficiency and we distinguish the professor from the apprentice. The qualifications are plain clothes, old shoes, an eye for nature, good humor, vast curiosity, good speech, good silence, and nothing too much. Good observers have the manners of trees and animals, and if they add words, 'tis only when words are better than silence. But a vain talker profanes the rivers and the forest, and is nothing like so good company as a dog."

Out of doors, all of our senses are fully rewarded. Our eyes are grateful for the long views and for the color and beauty of growing things, for clouds, rocks, and earth. Our ears are filled with the enchantment of small sounds and songs instead of with harsh noises, and our noses wrinkle with delight at the smell of pine needles in the hot sun, sweet earth and moss, and gray sage. All the time our feet are carrying us forward, our senses of sight and hearing and smell are lingering along the way, holding fast to the picture, making it into a memory.

Inexperienced hikers should set their goal at a reasonable distance. Training and preparation by taking a number of short hikes are necessary before taking a long hike.

Your first tramp will probably be a walk from the end of a car or bus line to an attractive spot in the suburbs of your town. A Friday afternoon hike after school to some point nearby, where you can watch the sunset as you eat your supper out of doors, is easy to arrange. After a number of short tramps, take a longer hike, perhaps an all-day trip. As you grow more accustomed to walking and more familiar with trails your hikes may grow longer and more adventurous.

## HITTING THE TRAIL

Wherever you live in this country, you should be able to choose an attractive spot as the goal of your hike and hike to it through interesting country.

Walk with a free and easy stride, swinging your arms. If you point your toes straight ahead, Indian fashion, you will not only cover more distance at each step but will not tire so quickly, for your weight will be carried on the outer half of the foot, where it can best be born. Be sure to walk with your head and chest up, so that your lungs and heart can do their work.

Never try to set a speed record. The joy of the trail is not in the distance covered but in the scenes, adventures, and discoveries along the way. Three miles an hour is a good average speed after you get started and into the swing of it.

If the way leads along an automobile highway or traveled road, walk on the left side of the road, facing oncoming traffic. This rule is a law in several states. It is best always to step off a narrow or busy road at the approach of vehicles. When walking on a public highway at night, a white scarf or a white handkerchief tied about the arm should be worn, so that one may be seen by motorists.

Avoid all doubtful areas that may be boggy or otherwise dangerous. Never walk along railroad tracks or trestles. To do so is trespassing as well as incurring grave risk to your safety.

## REST ALONG THE WAY

It is a good plan to rest for five or ten minutes about once every hour while you are tramping. If you go at an even, not too rapid pace, you will not, as a rule, need to rest more often unless you are unaccustomed to hiking or are hiking in hilly country or mountains. The best way to rest is to lie flat on your back, with legs raised and propped against a tree or rock, so that the circulation will be carried away from the feet. Be sure to rest on a poncho, sweater, or blanket if the ground is damp. Try this "rest exercise": lie on your back, raise your feet over your head, and imitate the pedaling of a bicycle.

## WHEN YOU ARE THIRSTY

Most experienced trampers drink little water while on foot. An orange or a lemon is good to suck when you are thirsty.

## KEEP YOUR EYES OPEN ON THE TRAIL

Wonder lies along the trail, no matter what kind of country you are hiking through. Perhaps you are curious to know some of the shy furred and feathered creatures that make their homes within sight of the trail. Many birds and animals are too shy to readily become friendly, but it is interesting to watch them quietly and carefully. Birds, wood mice and wood rats, bats, rabbits, squirrels, foxes, opossums, raccoons, weasels, moles, gophers, chipmunks, woodchucks, beavers, frogs, toads, lizards, and snakes may be seen on a hike. Girls in some parts of the country may have the thrilling adventure of seeing larger animals such as bears, deer, coyotes, and even moose, elk, puma, wild cats, and bison.

Domestic animals, too, are met on the trail. Remember that strange dogs and cats should be approached slowly, so that you may see whether they are friendly before they are within reach. Dogs frequently have a sense of duty toward the farmhouses or places where they live and may be perfectly justified in their prejudices against strangers.

Though most horses and cattle are harmless, when you are crossing fields or pastures it is best to be discreet and stay near a fence. Then you may quickly climb over or through it in case it's necessary. Sometimes horses or cattle are unfriendly and aggressive; according to a famous big-game hunter, the domestic bull is the most dangerous animal in North America. Where there is a cunning tiny calf to play with and to pet, remember there is usually a cow within call which might not care to find you meddling with her offspring. Some horses resent attention to their colts, also.

Denizens of the countryside that are interesting to know of are the skunk and the porcupine, both of which will leave you alone unless they are molested. The porcupine has prickly quills, which are barbed like fish-hooks and cause much pain if they penetrate the flesh. The skunk is about the size of a cat and is usually black with wide white stripes or spots down its back. When attacked or frightened it may give off an oil spray that has such a penetrating odor that it is almost unbearable to both man and beast. A skunk or a porcupine, however, may also make an interesting pet.

Most girls know enough about bees and wasps to be careful while watching them. Papery wasp nests on a branch, in the ground, or under the roof of a dwelling, with wasps passing in and out, are best left alone.

The friendly daddy-long-legs, often mistaken for a spider but only a near relative of true spiders, is quite harmless. Of the true spiders, there are two which should be known and avoided. One is black, about the size of a marble, and found in dark places such as sheds, outhouses, and under bridges. It is generally found throughout the country and may be readily recognized by a bright red or yellow hour-glass-shaped spot on the under side of its body which is round and shiny, not velvety like most spiders. The other poisonous spiders belong to the tarantula family. They are large and hairy, live in holes in the ground, and are found in the southwestern part of our country.

Snakes also may be met on the trail. Unless you know the dangerous snakes of your locality, it is best to leave all snakes alone.

## PRINCIPLES OF HAPPY HIKING

The first of them is to *prepare well.*
Have some reasonable idea of where it is that you are hiking.
Perhaps a map and compass (or GPS) would be in order.
Get your stuff together, but don't pack anything you can just as
well do without. Do plan on carrying some water.
Tell someone where it is you think you are going and when you
expect to return.
Hydrate.
Finish getting your gear together, and head out.
The second of them is to *hike safely.*
Don't take silly chances or push things too hard. Show a little
common sense and personal discipline that are the foundations of
a safe and happy trek.
The third is to *leave no sign that you were ever there.*
Leave no litter of any kind along your way. If you pack it in, you
pack it out.
Do no damage of any kind. Don't pick the flowers or over-handle
the foliage.
Practice silence.

## SNAKES, GOOD AND BAD

Snakes are to the animal world what toadstools are to the vegetable world—wonderful things, beautiful things, but fearsome things because some of them are deadly poison.

These poisonous snakes may be divided into three groups: Coral Snakes, Moccasins, and Rattlers.

The Coral Snakes are found in the Southern States. They are very much like harmless snakes in shape but are easily distinguished by their remarkable colors, "broad alternating rings of red and black, the latter bordered with very narrow rings of yellow."

The Rattlesnakes are readily told at once by the rattle.

But the Moccasins are not so easy to identify. There are two kinds: the water moccasin, or cottonmouth, found in South Carolina, Georgia, Florida, Alabama, and Louisiana; and the copperhead, which is also known as the highland, northern moccasin, or pilot snake, found from Massachusetts to Florida and west to Illinois and Texas.

Here are distinguishing marks: The moccasins, as well as the rattlers, have on each side of the head between the eye and nostril, a deep pit.

The pupil of the eye is an upright line, like a cat's; the harmless snakes have a round pupil.

The moccasins have a single row of plates under the tail, while the harmless snakes have a double row.

The water moccasin is dull olive with wide, black transverse bands.

The copperhead is dull hazel brown, marked across the back with dumbbells of reddish brown; the top of the head is more or less coppery.

Both moccasins and rattlers have a flat triangular head, which is much wider than the thin neck, while most harmless snakes have a narrow head that shades off into the neck.

Rattlesnakes are found generally distributed all over the United States, southern Ontario, southern Alberta, and Saskatchewan.

## HOW DOES A SNAKE BITE?

Remember, the tongue is a feeler, not a stinger. The "stinging" is done by two long, hollow teeth, or fangs, through which the poison is squirted into the wound.

The striking distance of a snake is about one-third the creature's length, and the stroke is so swift that no creature can dodge it.

The snake can strike farthest and surest when it is ready coiled but can strike a little way when travelling.

You cannot disarm a poisonous snake without killing it. If the fangs are removed others come quickly to take their place. In fact, a number of small, half-grown fangs are always waiting, ready to be developed.

## IN CASE OF SNAKE BITE

First, keep cool, and remember that the bite of American snakes is seldom fatal if the proper measures are followed.

You must act at once. Try to keep the poison from getting into the system by a tight bandage on the arm or leg (it is sure to be one or the other) just above the wound. Next, get the poison out of the wound by slashing the wound two or more ways with a sharp knife or razor at least as deep as the puncture. Squeeze it—wash it out. Suck it out with the lips (if you have no wounds in the mouth it will do you no harm there). Work, massage, suck, and wash to get all the poison out. After thorough treatment to remove the venom, the ligature may be removed.

Pack small bits of gauze into the wounds to keep them open and draining, then dress over them with gauze saturated with any good antiseptic solution. Keep the dressing saturated and the wounds open for at least a week, no matter how favorable the symptoms.

## HARMLESS SNAKES

The greatest number of our snakes are harmless, beautiful, and beneficent. They are friendly to the farmer because, although some destroy a few birds, chickens, ducklings, and game, the largest part of their food are mice and insects. The black snake, the milk snake, and one or two others will bite in self-defense, but they have no poisonous fangs, and the bite is much like the prick of a bramble.

TYPES OF POISONOUS SNAKES:

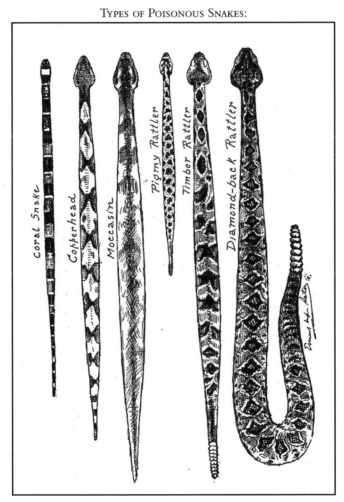

ILLUS. FROM WOODCRAFT MANUAL FOR GIRLS

## STALKING, TRACKING, AND TRAILING

Hikers need not follow a man-made track. There are several ways to travel across country without following a trail or getting lost. You may wish to tramp along the bank of a stream or follow a ridge of hills or explore a ravine or water course. A telephone cross-country wire is usually the shortest possible route between two points and may be interesting to follow, if a sharp lookout is kept for branching or crossing telephone lines. It is not only fun to hike by such guides but it is well to know them, should you happen to get lost. The telephone wires sooner or later come to a town, and the stream usually passes by a camp or a roadway, while from a ridge of hills you may watch for landmarks or smoke and so find your way again.

A road cut through the woods and long since overgrown and forgotten is fascinating to trace and follow. It may lead to a house, weather-beaten and falling apart; it may lead to an abandoned mine or quarry; or it may end in an old lumber camp. You should explore only the outside of unused mines or caves, except when accompanied by an expert guide.

Stalking is the art of following an animal without being noticed, so that you may observe the animal's natural behavior or discover its intentions. It is also of particular value in animal photography.

## *ANIMAL TRACKS*

There is a fascinating language in animal tracks. After a snowfall, it often surprises us to find in our own yards messages from passing creatures.

The footprints of animals teach us a great deal about the way in which they live and from them we may learn to read many an interesting story.

The cat and members of the cat family may draw their claws in and out whenever they wish, and their tracks show only "pads" and no claw marks.

The dog's and fox's claws are always in sight and show in their tracks in addition to the pads.

The footprints of bears, raccoons, and skunks are called plantigrade tracks because the greater portion of the animal's foot is shown in the track. The plantigrade animals are called flatfooted.

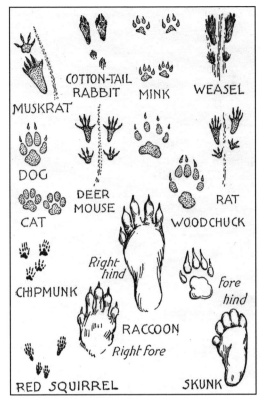

SOME FAMILIAR ANIMAL TRACKS

Footprints of animals such as deer, sheep, moose, and elk may be called hoofed tracks.

Bird tracks differ according to whether the birds are tree perchers, ground walkers, or water birds. The tree percher hops along, both feet in line. For an example of this, notice sparrow tracks in the dust or snow. The ground walker puts one foot down, then the other. Hen tracks and the tracks of the partridge show this characteristic. The waddlers, water birds like the duck and goose, walk in a pigeon-toed fashion.

In studying tracks it is important to know how old they are. The state of the ground and the weather affect the track. On a dry windy day a track on light sandy soil looks old in a very short time because any damp earth that may be kicked up from under the surface dries very rapidly to the same color as the surface dust. The same track on damp ground looks much fresher because the sun has only partially dried the upturned soil. If the track is on clay, under the shade of trees where the sun does not get at it, the same print which may have looked a day old in the sand here looks quite fresh.

A clue to the age of tracks is often found in rain spots which may have fallen on them since they were made (if it is known at what time the rain fell), dust or grass seeds blown into them (if it is known at what time the wind was blowing), the crossing of other tracks over the original ones, or the extent to which grass that has been trodden down has dried or withered. In following a horse, the length of time since it passed may also be judged by the freshness of the droppings, due allowance being made for the effect of sun and rain upon them.

## DESIGNING YOUR HIKE

The following kinds of hikes are suggestive of many other ways in which you may plan an expedition.

### TREASURE HIKE

Lay a trail ending with a treasure, which may consist of a lunch or sweets.

### EXPLORATION HIKE

Plan a hike through unfamiliar country so that you will have a chance to explore, each with the possibility of making interesting and surprising discoveries. Pretend that you are the first explorers of the region; observe landmarks and the lay of the land; make a map that is accurate enough for another party of explorers to follow.

### ZIGZAG HIKE

At the first crossroad, turn right; at the second, turn left; and so forth. More interesting things are likely to be found on the byways than on the highways. A snack-size lunch should be carried because of the uncertainty of finding a suitable place in which to cook or to prepare food.

### TRACKING AND TRAILING HIKE

Plan games in which one patrol stalks another.

### POINT TO POINT HIKE

Choose a goal from a half-mile to two miles away. (It is best to avoid a course that crosses streams.) The players should go directly to the goal without going around obstacles—such as clumps of bushes, rocks, or fences. They should go straight ahead, over, or through obstacles without turning to the left or right for any reason. Each girl is penalized one point for every yard or foot she goes to the right or left. The one who reaches the goal with the fewest points wins the game. This game should be played where you will not disturb or intrude upon neighbors or run any personal risks, like getting wet in a stream or meeting an unfriendly animal in a pasture.

### STORY HIKE

Use a story such as *Treasure Island, Peter Pan and Wendy*, or *Alice's Adventures in Wonderland* to illustrate a hike. Lay a trail using phrases and places from the story.

### HISTORICAL HIKE

Choose an historical landmark as your goal and know the story of it before going on the hike. Almost every nook and corner of this country has its own fascinating bit of history to be re-told in pageant, song, verse, dramatic presentation, or by word-of-mouth. What happened in your part of the country in pioneer days? Are there nearby hills where Indians burned signal fires? Is there a valley where a council was held between frontiersmen and redmen? What explorers or American settlers first came to your region?

### STAR-GAZING HIKE

Choose a moonless night for the study of the stars.

### PIONEER HIKE

Improvise equipment necessary for cooking an outdoor meal along the way or at the campsite. Carry no equipment from the home base.

*CITY HIKE*

If you live in a big city where it is difficult to get out into the country, you may have a city hike. Take a trip to a museum, an aquarium, a zoological or botanical garden, or even to a market, where you will find many fascinating fruits and vegetables which originally came from foreign corners of the earth. A visit to a ship in a harbor fuels the imagination. In many a city or town, a history of the land may be read in excavations for new buildings, where the exposed earth shows the layers of rock and sand and soil upon which pavements and buildings are placed.

*FOLLOWING THE MAP HIKE*

Get a United States geological survey map of your region and take a hike by reading the map, tramping across country as far as possible. Indicate on the map the trail followed and all points of particular interest: rare trees, rock foundations, or other landmarks. Mounting such a map on cloth is a good way to prepare for the hike in troop meeting. The use of the compass may be practised on this hike.

## SIXTY-FOUR COMMON WILD FLOWERS

### OF THE UNITED STATES AND SOUTHERN CANADA

The Adventurous Girl is advised to color each flower from nature as the opportunity occurs, using water colors over the outline given. They are grouped here to correspond with the eight plates.

### BLUE FLOWERS

Liverleaf or Hepatica (*Hepatica triloba*). A lovely lilac or blue, the first of the spring flowers in most regions. It blooms in the woods from March to May, from Nova Scotia to Manitoba, and southward.

Blue-eyed Grass, Blue Star, or Star Grass (*Sisyrinchium angustifolium*). A bright blue flower of the Iris family; found in rich meadows from Newfoundland to British Columbia and southward halfway to the Gulf; it blooms from May to August.

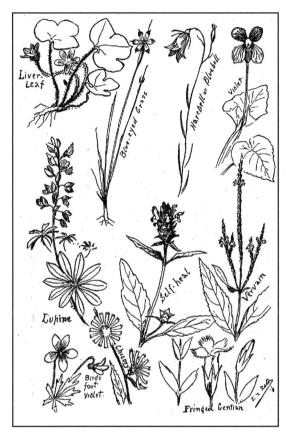

BLUE FLOWERS

Bluebell, Harebell, or Hairbell (*Campanula rotundifolia*). Found on rocky places and uplands nearly everywhere south of the middle states. It blooms all summer.

Common Violet, or Heartsease (*Viola cuccullata*). The leaf's heart shape was held to be the proof of its power to set the heart at ease. It's found in rich ground, Nova Scotia to Minnesota and southward nearly to the Gulf States. Blooms in spring.

Bird's foot Violet (*Viola pedata*). So called from the shape of its leaves. It's found in dry ground, from Maine to Minnesota and southward.

Lupine (*Lupinus perennis*). It's found in dry soil, from Maine to Minnesota and southward in the early summer.

Self-heal, or Heal-all (*Prunella vulgaris*). It can be found in dry ground everywhere; it blooms from May to October.

Vervain, Blue Vervain, or Wild Hyssop (*Verbena hastata*). It is found in moist ground everywhere; it blooms from June to September.

Chicory, or Succory (*Chicorium Intybus*). The flowers are bright blue or sometimes white. The roots roasted and ground make a wholesome substitute for coffee. These flowers originally came here from Europe and are now found generally in the Eastern U. S. It blooms from July to October.

Fringed Gentian (*Gentiana crinita*). Bright blue; rarely white. It is found in rich meadows, from Quebec to Minnesota and southward halfway to the Gulf. It blooms in September and October.

## WHITE FLOWERS

Bloodroot (*Sanguinaria Canadensis*). Noted for bleeding when cut, its root furnished the Indians with a red paint. It's found in rich woods, from Nova Scotia to Manitoba and southward, and blooms April and May.

May Apple, or Wild Mandrake (*Podophyllum peltatum*). It's found in low woods in southern Ontario to Minnesota and southward. It flowers in May and the fruit is ripe in July or August and is very wholesome.

Starflower (*Trientalis americana*). This flower is found in damp woods from Labrador westward and south to the Middle States, and blooms in May and June.

Indian Pipe (*Monotropa uniflora*). It's found in rich woods in nearly all of the U. S. and southern Canada. It blooms from June to August. The whole plant is white or occasionally pink.

Saxifrage (*Saxifraga Virginiensis*). It grows in dry, rocky woods, from New Brunswick to Minnesota and southward to Georgia. One of the early flowers of spring, it blooms March to May.

Ox-eye Daisy (*Chrysanthemum Leucanthemum*). It can be found in pastures throughout most of the area as a troublesome weed from Europe. It's in bloom May to November. White rays surround a bright yellow disk on this flower.

Big White Trillium, or Wake-robin (*Trillium grandiflorum*). This flower is found in the woods from Quebec to Minnesota and southward. It's typically found blooming in May and June.

Boneset (*Eupatorium perfoliatum*). It is found in wet places from New Brunswick to Manitoba and southward. It blooms from July to September and the flowers are white, but sometimes blue.

## PINK, OR WHITE STREAKED WITH PINK

Trailing Arbutus (*Epigœa repens*). Found in sandy or rocky woods, this flower is generally distributed in eastern America. It blooms in spring, from March to May.

Twin-flower (*Linnea borealis*). It's typically found in the cold woods of the northern half of the continent and southward along the high mountains and blooms from June to August.

Spring Beauty (*Claytonia Virginica*). This flower is found in moist wood throughout eastern America and blooms March to May.

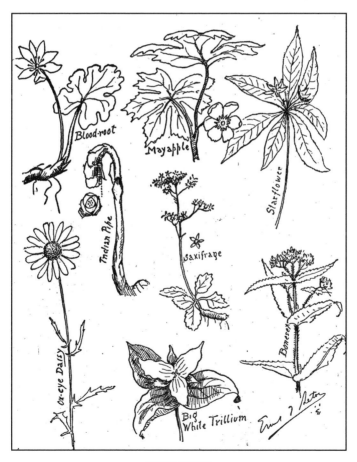

WHITE FLOWERS

Queen Orchid, or Showy Ladies Slipper (*Cypripedium reginae*). It's found in swamps from Nova Scotia to Minnesota and south to Georgia. It blooms June to September.

Purple Moccasin Flower (*Cypripedium acaule*). It's found in sandy or rocky woods from Newfoundland to Minnesota and south to the middle states. It blooms in May and June.

Rose Pink (*Sabbatia angularis*). Found in rich soil from New York to Ontario and south to the Gulf states, this flower blooms July and August.

Showy Orchis (*Orchis spectabilis*). It's found in rich woods from New Brunswick to Minnesota and southward to the middle states. It blooms in April and June. The flowers are violet or purple streaked with white or light purple.

PINK OR WHITE STREAKED WITH PINK

Mountain Laurel (*Kalmia latifolia*). This flower grows in sandy or rocky woods from New Brunswick to Ontario, and southward. It blooms in May and June.

Pink Azalea (*Azalea nudiflora*). It's found in dry woods from Maine to Illinois and southward. It blooms in April and May.

## WHITE, OR GREENISH-WHITE FLOWERS

Plantain, Ribgrass, or Whiteman's Foot (*Plantago major*). This flower can be found everywhere in our region and blooms all summer long as well as in the spring.

Queen Anne's Lace, or Wild Carrot (*Daucus carota*). It's found everywhere; brought from Europe and known as "the original of the cultivated carrot," it blooms all summer.

Yarrow, or Milfoil (*Achillea Millefolium*). It's widely distributed and blooms from June to November.

Grass of Parnassus (*Parnassia Caroliniana*). It's found in low meadows in New Brunswick and Manitoba and southward to the middle states. It blooms June to September.

Solomon's Seal (*Polygonalum biflorum*). It grows in the woods from New Brunswick to Ontario and southward. Blooming from April to July, its roots show a seal-like impression, hence the name.

False Solomon's Seal, Wild Spikenard, or Zigzag (*Vagnera racemosa*). Found in the U. S. and south Canada generally, it blooms May to July.

Stickweed, Cleavers, or Bedstraw (*Galium mollugo*). Generally distributed in fields in the Northeastern States, it flowers all summer long. There is also one with a yellow flower.

Pennsylvania or Canada Anemone (*Anemone Canadensis*). Found from Labrador to the Plains and southward to Kansas on low ground, it blooms all summer.

Wind flower (*Anemone quinquifolia*). It's found in low woods, generally east of the Rockies. One of the early spring flowers, it blooms from April to June.

Rue Anemone (*Syndesmon thalictroides*). Found in woods from the Atlantic to Minnesota and south to Kansas, this flower is sometimes white, but often pinkish. One of the earliest spring flowers, it blooms from March to June.

## YELLOW FLOWERS

Celandine (*Chelidonium majus*). A straggler from Europe is now common along roadsides in eastern U. S. It blooms April to September. Its juice is a strong yellow dye.

Black-eyed Susan or Cone-flower (*Rudbeckea hirta*). It's found in fields from Quebec to the Plains and southward. It blooms May to September.

Yellow Star-grass (*Hypoxis hirsuta*). It's found in dry soil from Maine to the Plains and southward. It blooms May to October.

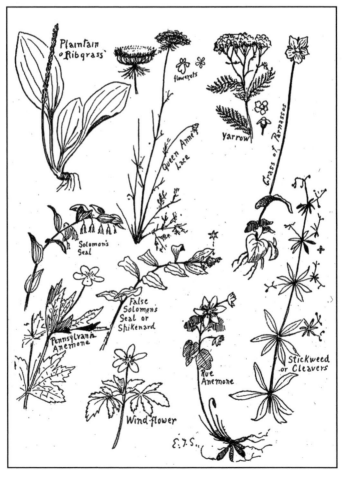

WHITE OR GREENISH WHITE FLOWERS

Jewelweed, Touch-me-not, or Silverleaf (*Impatiens biflora*). This flower grows in moist ground from Nova Scotia to Alaska and southward and blooms July to October.

Yellow Toadflax or Butter and Eggs (*Linaria Linaria*). It's found in dry waste places from Nova Scotia to Manitoba and south to the middle states and blooms from June to October.

Evening Primrose (*Onagra biennis*). It's found in dry soil from Labrador to the Rockies and south to Florida. It blooms from June to October and opens typically at night.

Adder's Tongue or Dog-tooth Violet (*Erythronium Americanum*). It grows in moist woods from Nova Scotia to Minnesota and southward. One of the earliest spring flowers, it blooms from March to May. The

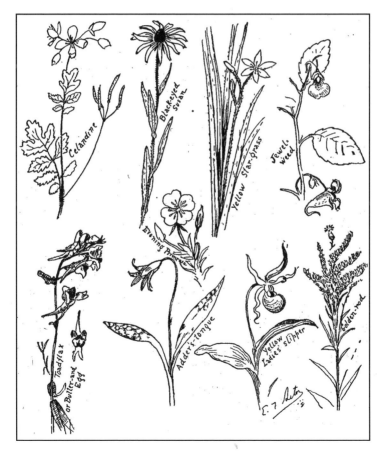

YELLOW FLOWERS

name was possibly once "Adderstung," from the blotched appearance of the leaves.

Yellow Lady's Slipper (*Cypripedium hirsutum*). It's found in woods from Newfoundland to British Columbia and southward at least to the Middle States. A smaller variety is also recognized and it blooms from May to July.

Goldenrod (*Solidago Canadensis*). Found from the Atlantic to the Plains and southward, this is the emblem flower of America. It blooms from August to November. There are some fifty species of Goldenrod recognized in America, so it is expert work to classify them all.

## RED, PURPLE, OR SCARLET FLOWERS

Cardinal Flower (*Lobelia cardinalis*). It's found in moist soil from New Brunswick to the Plains and southward. It blooms July to September and is a brilliant red or scarlet, rarely white.

Red Lily or Wood Lily (*Lilium Philadelphicum*). It grows in dry woods, from Maine to Manitoba and southward to the middle states. It blooms in June and July.

Turk's Cap Lily (*Lilium superbum*). Found in wet meadows from Maine to Minnesota and southward halfway to the Gulf, this flower blooms in July and August.

Columbine (*Aquilegia Canadensis*). It's found in rocky woods from Nova Scotia to the Plains and southward. It blooms April to July.

Fire Pink (*Silene Virginica*). It grows in dry woods from New York to Minnesota and southward to the middle states. It blooms May to September.

Painted Cup or Indian Paint-brush (*Castilleja coccinea*). Found in moist meadows from Maine to Manitoba and southward halfway to the Gulf, it blooms from May to July. The flowers are yellowish and inconspicuous; the scarlet is chiefly on the upper l eaves.

Pitcher Plant (*Sarracenia purpurea*). In peat bogs from Labrador to the Rockies and southward up high, it blooms in May and June.

Bee Balm or Oswego Tea (*Monarda didyma*). It is found in moist soil in the east from Ontario to Georgia. It blooms in July and September.

Redcap or Purple Flowering Raspberry (*Rubus odoratus*). Found on the edge of woods from Nova Scotia to Michigan and southward halfway to the Gulf, this flower blooms from June to August. Its blooms

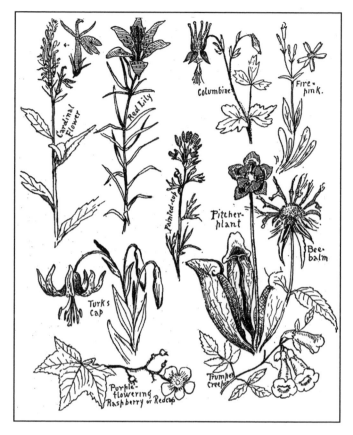

RED PURPLE OR SCARLET FLOWERS

are worth far more than its berry, which is a thin red cap of fine gravel held together with a little fruit pulp.

Trumpet Creeper (*Tecoma radicans*). It grows in moist woods from New Jersey to Illinois and southward to Texas. It blooms in August and September.

## BROWNISH PURPLE FLOWERS

Wild Ginger (*Asarum Canadense*). It's found in rich woods from New Brunswick to Manitoba and southward halfway to the Gulf. It blooms in April and May. Its roots are flavored like ginger.

Jack-in-the-pulpit or Indian Turnip (*Arisaema triphyllium*). It's found in moist woods from Nova Scotia to Minnesota and southward to the

Gulf States. Its root is frightfully acrid and pungent when raw but when boiled becomes a wholesome food.

Red Trillium or Smelly Wake-robin (*Trillium erectum*). It grows in the woods from Nova Scotia to James' Bay and Manitoba, then southward halfway to the Gulf. Its color varies from dark purple to pink, green, or white. It blooms from April to June. The name Wake-robin is supposed to mean that it wakes when the robin comes. It has a very bad smell and as a consequence country boys call it by simple, sincere, but very vernacular names.

Skunk Cabbage (*Spathyema foetida*). It grows in swamps from Nova Scotia to Minnesota and southward to the Gulf States. Its bloom is the first of all the spring flowers, in moist localities, for it sends its big egg-shaped and purple-mottled bloom into the cold world as early as February, long before its leaves will venture forth. In March and April it is still in flower.

## PINK FLOWERS

Wild Geranium or Crane's Bill (*Geranium maculatum*). It's found in woods from Newfoundland to Manitoba and southward nearly to the

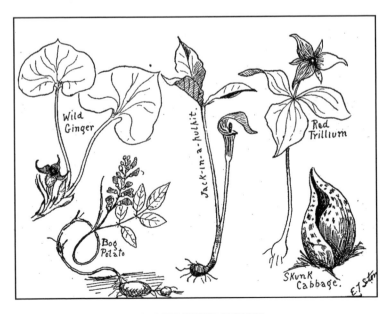

BROWNISH PURPLE FLOWERS

Gulf. It blooms from April to July. The name Crane's Bill comes from the shape of the seed pod.

Fire Weed, Epilobium, or Spiked Willowherb (*Chamaenerion angustifolium*). It's found in dry sunny places from Labrador to Alaska and southward at least halfway to the Gulf. So called because of its commonly springing up after a forest fire, this flower blooms June to September.

Milkweed (*Asclepias purpurascens*). Found in dry sunny places from Massachusetts to Minnesota and southward halfway to the Gulf, it blooms June to August.

Spotted Pipsissiwa (*Chimaphila maculata*). It grows in dry woods from Maine to Minnesota and southward nearly to the Gulf States. It blooms June to August.

## MOUNTAIN CLIMBING

*By Eloise Roorbach, 1912*

Mountain climbing is the final test of an Adventurous Girl's perseverance in following a trail and also in endurance, courage, and woodcraftmanship. Nature reserves her choicest beauties and secrets for those who know how to conquer all difficulties. No girl's education is complete until she has seen mountain peaks with white snow, piercing the blue sky as far as the eye can see and clouds forming below her feet, breathed rare air found only in high places, drank from the pure source of rivers, and heard the mighty roar of waterfalls. A climb to a high mountain top is an experience

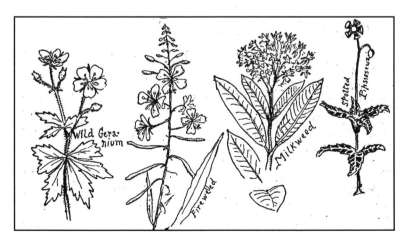

PINK FLOWERS

that will enrich and influence the entire life of whoever has had the hardiness and wisdom to accomplish it.

Before attempting this, the girl must be in perfect physical shape, be able to sleep on the ground, and has learned to live simply. Girls should train for this experience by taking gradually more difficult hikes. On these hikes the girls can practice using the condensed foods that must be depended upon in mountain climbing. The rations for those who wish to climb to high places must necessarily be limited, for each girl must carry her own rations for two weeks.

The foundation of a mountain climber's food supply is rice, bacon, cheese, chocolate, raisins, dates, dried fruits, powdered soups, whole wheat crackers, and tea. *Tea should be used instead of coffee.* The chocolate is sometimes made into a refreshing drink. Only a small amount of sugar and salt can be carried. This fare is augmented by mushrooms, wild fruit and berries, and fish. Some hardened climbers add a little "jerky" (dried meat) to these staples as well.

No definite rule of distance to be covered in a day can be laid down. In the high mountains, ten or twelve miles of hiking a day should be considered a maximum, for part of the benefit to be gained from such a trip is the enjoyment of the trip itself. It is better to go a few miles slowly, observing keenly all the time, stopping for frequent rests to examine a flower, to drink at a clear spring, or to feast upon the view than to cover more ground in a hurried way.

The following is a suggestion for the management of a day in high mountain altitudes. Arise with the sun or a little before breakfast. Breakfast consists of rice, dried fruit (put to soak the night before), bacon, and shredded wheat biscuit. Before packing, make a small package of cheese, chocolate, raisins, and a biscuit for the noon lunch that can be reached without having to unpack equipment. There should be a rest of at least an hour at noon, eating slowly, throwing off the pack, and, if possible, relaxing flat on the back for a while. Then another hike of three or four miles, making camp early in the evening, about five o'clock. This divides the day into two periods of hikes with a rest in between. The dinner is like the breakfast, with the addition of soup. Soup can be prepared and eaten while the rice is cooking. Mountain trout can also be fried with bacon.

The equipment must be as light as possible. Clothing should consist of one pair of stout, high, waterproof boots, one pair of light moccasins for in the camp, shorts, sturdy pants, hat, gauntlet gloves, one change of underclothes, three pairs of wool stockings, one sweater, one comb (no brush), one small pocket mirror, ivory soap or soap leaves, one tube of cold cream, compass, fishing rod, lines and hooks, rope, stout string, notebook and map, small hatchet, and matches (in a waterproof case).

No guns, books, or cameras can be carried on a high hike, for their weight is prohibitive. A sleeping bag made of eiderdown, lined with canton flannel, and covered with oiled silk or duck's back can be rolled and carried across the shoulders. A knife, fork, and spoon, in addition to the big sheath knife worn at the belt, one frying pan, tin plate and cup (aluminum should be used in preference as tin rusts easily), and a rice and a soup kettle are all the cooking utensils needed. If a girl attempts a high mountain climb, additional layers of clothing and more food can be carried on a pack mule, but this chapter is for those who wish to climb unencumbered with pack animals. It is by far the finest way to see the high mountains, though it must be admitted few have the gumption or courage to try it.

## CAMPING

### THE SITE

The essential points to be considered in selecting a site for an overnight camp are highlighted in this section.

The water supply must come from a source known to be pure, there must be an ample supply of firewood or other fuel, and the ground upon which you are to sleep must be dry. The site should be elevated above its surroundings so that there is natural drainage and no danger of being flooded by the sudden rise of a stream. It should have direct sunlight during some part of the day. In some parts of the country where sudden changes in weather may be experienced, shelter must be within reach. This shelter may be permanent or it may be temporarily constructed from ponchos or by pitching tents. If temporary shelter is used it is generally advisable to dig a trench along the outer wall which leads into a lower level, to provide for drainage.

The campfire should have the first consideration. It should be near the water and should have open ground space, without trees nearby or low branches overhanging. Usually there should be a windbreak as well.

When you arrive at the camp, no matter how late it is or how hungry you are, spread your bed on a poncho and cover with a poncho to guard against dew until bedtime unless tents are used, in which case they should be erected first. You can cook and eat supper quite easily by the firelight, but you should have daylight, if possible, by which to select a place to sleep and to arrange your bed. Then, too, if you wait until sleepiness actually overtakes you before spreading your blankets on the ground, you will probably find yourself in the lumpiest spot the region affords. Choose above all else a level spot, or one that has the barest perceptible incline up toward where you will put your head.

Many years' accumulation of pine or redwood needles or good grass turf affords the best outdoor mattresses. Stones and bits of wood must be removed and partly buried roots avoided when selecting a place to sleep. When a desirable spot cannot be found because of great masses of rocks, or if the ground is hard, sunbaked clay, a mattress or twigs or leaves may be used.

Beds should be comfortable and safe. There are times and places when it is better to sleep on a folding cot than on the ground, especially if the ground is wet or if frequent heavy showers are to be expected. There are areas where sand burs and other weeds are very hard on both the bedding and the sleeper, and in some regions chiggers, creeping things, or snakes make cots or hammocks a necessity. There are camping places in the United States where the only way to be insured against ants is to put the legs of the cot in cans of water.

Be sure to cast an eye overhead to see that the branches of overspreading trees are not dead or rotten and about to fall, and do not make your bed where there is danger of having stones roll down on you or where a member of the party may step off an embankment in the darkness.

When your bed is spread ready to crawl into, stow your toilet articles and clothes away neatly, either under a poncho or under your blankets.


## HOW TO USE KNIVES, AXES, AND HACHETS

The proper use of knives, hatchets, or axes is a sign of a good woodswoman. They are carried for use, not for play. They are kept in good condition, clean and sharp, and are used in such a way that neither the user nor anyone nearby may be injured by them.

*In Using a Knife:*

- Whittle or cut away from the body.
- Keep the fingers behind the blade.
- Do not carry an open knife in your hand.
- Keep the knife clean; boil or scald the blades before cutting food with them; keep the knife out of the fire.
- Know how to sharpen the blades properly and how to keep them sharp. A dull knife is harder to handle than a sharp one.

## USING AN AX OR HATCHET

In carrying an ax or hatchet, always protect the blade with a sheath or guard. Carry an ax by grasping the handle close to the ax head with the blade down and outward.

In chopping, see that a clear space encircles you, both around and above you. The chopper is responsible for others who may pass by.

When chopping down a tree, a branch, or a sapling with an ax, take pains to cut away all the twigs and foliage so that the ax will not touch anything when it is swung. Even a small twig may deflect it and cause an injury.

Always chop wood in such a position that the ax or hatchet will not strike the body if it should slip.

Always use a low, solid stationary chopping block or log as a base when splitting wood or kindling.

Do not hold a stick of wood in one hand and chop with the other.

Be sure that the head of an ax or hatchet is on firmly.

## SHELTERS

When sleeping outside for several days or in bad weather, some kind of shelter is needed. The best kind of temporary outdoor shelter for all kinds of weather is a good tent with a dry board floor. But this is usually found only in established camps. If campers or hikers must take their shelter with them and put it up, a tent such as the Andree hike tent or the Baker tent serves very well. Of course all heavy equipment such as tents and bedding must be transported by back to the camp site.

As soon as camp is reached, tents should be unpacked and set up. A level stretch of ground somewhat in the open should be selected. Unless it is slightly elevated so as to provide natural drainage, the ground must be well trenched to carry off the water if it rains. Otherwise water may collect at the tent edges and flow into the tent. A trench is necessary only in wet weather or in a climate where sudden showers are a possibility. Tent pegs hold best in gravelly soil. On very rocky or sandy ground, the four corners of the tent may have to be anchored by tying them to big rocks.

The lean-to is a useful shelter that may be built of branches and boughs, if permission has been secured to cut them. It is a good protection against wind. With a reflector fire built before it, it is warm and snug even in cold weather.

To make a lean-to, select two trees about eight feet apart. Lash a cross-pole to these trees at a height of about four feet. Lay sticks slantwise against the crossbar, so that they will make a roof against the wind. The lower end of each stick should be driven into the ground, the other end should be lashed to the bar. With evergreen boughs, or thickly-leaved branches or bark, thatch these cross-poles in lacing fashion, which is easier to do if bars are laid across the up and down poles. The sides of this shelter between the sloping thatch and the trees may be covered in the same manner.

If well lashed, the framework for this shelter will hold for a long time.

## FOOD STORAGE AND PRESERVATION

### *THE ORIOLE PANTRY*

To keep provisions away from animals, throw one end of a rope over a branch and fasten it to the handle of a basket or box or through the string tied around the food bag, and pull the perishable food up out of the sunshine and away from ground insects. The Andree pack basket is excellent for this purpose. Tie the tree end of the rope securely. The rope may be covered with flypaper for several inches above the hanging receptacle to keep away ants.

### *THE ANTI-ANT BOX*

In parts of the country where ants are pests, the legs of an improvised pantry should stand in cans of water. As soon as four cans of food have been emptied, partly fill them with water and insert the four legs of the pantry in them—four short sticks nailed or lashed to a box frame. Be careful that there are no leaves or twigs left in the water, to serve as a bridge for the ants.

### *WET CACHE*

Where there is a stream of cold water at the camp site, the butter and milk may be kept cool by anchoring them in the water with rocks placed around the containers to weigh them down. Take care that no sudden rising of the stream will play havoc with this larder.

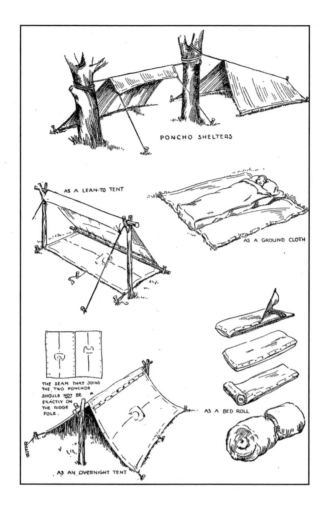

Where there is no stream a very satisfactory wet cache may be made by covering an orange crate or similar box with burlap, which is kept wet by allowing the ends of the burlap to soak in a pan of water placed on top of the box. The cache containing fresh vegetables and meat may be swung up out of reach of animals, as the oriole pantry described.

## DRY CACHE

Provisions such as butter and milk that must be kept cool should be stored in a dry cache if there is little danger of their being molested by animals and insects. Dig a pit two feet wide, two feet long, two feet deep, and line it with stones. Cut four sturdy poles, each long enough to reach across the pit, lash them together to form a square reinforced by smaller crosspieces. Weave green branches through the crosspieces to make a cover for the pit strong enough to keep an animal from falling through it. Be sure that the place is conspicuously marked, so that no one will stumble into it.

## SANITATION

In outdoor housekeeping, particular attention must be given to the disposal of all waste. All members of a camp should always use the agreed-upon latrine.

## LATRINE

A position for the latrine should be selected on a lower level than the source of the water supply, and at least one hundred yards from it. It should be constructed immediately upon arriving at the camp site and concealed by a thicket or improvised screens. One method of making the latrine is to dig a trench two feet long, twelve to eighteen inches wide, and a foot to a foot and a half deep. The earth excavated should be piled along the back of the trench. A whittled paddle or trowel should hang or stand nearby, and earth from the pile should be liberally sprinkled into the trench each time it is used. An empty tin may be used as a cover for the toilet paper. If a seat is desired, make one by driving stakes into the ground and lashing saplings across them. Before leaving the camp site burn brush in the trench if the surrounding area does not present a fire risk or throw the wood ashes left from the campfire into the trench; fill in with the remaining earth and leave as little trace of the excavation as possible.

## FIRE BUILDING

It is easy to build a safe fire in dry, still weather near the banks of a stream with plenty of dry tinder and matches. But if you can build a fire in pouring rain, when you have no dry tinder at all and only two matches left, you are a real camper.

Let "Safety First" be your watchwords while building and tending a fire. If you are careless you may not only lose your own equipment but also cause great loss of property to others—even loss of life.

The fire you make must depend upon many factors—the variety of wood and kindling at hand, weather conditions, the conditions of the immediate surroundings, the kind of fireplaces available, the kind of cooking you are going to do, and perhaps most important of all, the ability of the builders.

## WHERE TO BUILD A FIRE

- Build only small fires and select a site near water, if possible.
- Build the fire in the open, not against or under a tree or log.
- Scrape away all leaves and trash for at least ten feet all around the fire.
- Never leave the fire unattended.
- Extinguish the fire first with water, then cover with dirt. "Practically out" will not do; the fire must be completely out.

## TINDER AND WOOD FOR FIRES

Dead branches from the lower limbs of trees or standing wood are better for fire building than wood lying flat on the ground. They are more likely to be dry and less likely to be rotten. If the wood snaps when it is broken, it is good fuel. If it bends but does not break easily, it is too green. If it crumbles, it is rotten and without fuel value. Split wood burns better than whole logs.

Here are a few fire building pointers:

As the wood is gathered and cut, divide it into separate piles of tinder, kindling, and hard wood. A good camper should never have to go in search of wood after her fire is lighted. Sticks a foot long are better than smaller pieces because fire burns upward.

To start a fire, take a small forked stick about six inches in length and insert it in the ground at about a forty-five degree angle with the forked end out. Drop a handful of tinder over this. The forked stick will keep the tinder elevated and allow for air. Any type of fire may then be constructed. A bundle of dry plant stalks about a foot long, broken in half, and placed in a vertical position is a good starter.

## HOW TO LIGHT A MATCH IN THE WIND

*"Face the wind. Cup your hands, with their backs toward the wind, and hold the match with its head pointing toward the rear of the cup—i.e., toward the wind. Remove the right hand just long enough to strike the match on something very close by; then instantly resume the former position. The flames will run up the match stick, instead of being blown away from it, and so will have something to feed on."*

If light, dry tinder cannot be found, whittle fuzz sticks with which to start the fire. Select three or four short, dry sticks about as thick as a thumb and whittle thin shavings toward the end of the stick, but do not cut them entirely away from the stick. If it is raining split open a log and use splintered bits of the dry interior.

When necessary to conserve heat, lay the fire and hang the kettle before lighting, in order to get the most from the fire.

Cooking over coals is always more successful than cooking over flames. The food cooks more slowly, is more likely to be well done, and is less likely to burn. It is also possible to get closer to the fire without being burned. Kettles do not burn black over coals.

On a windy day build a small fire in a hole or trench and clear from around it, to an area fifteen to thirty feet in diameter, all inflammable material that may catch sparks.

### FIRE DESIGN

#### WIGWAM FIRE

*Purpose*: To boil quickly and to start other types of fires.

*Method*: Stand three fuzz sticks or a bunch of dry grass in a tripod and build around them a wigwam of sticks varying from the size of a match to the width of your finger. Feed the fire with small sticks as needed. A crane is frequently used with this fire.

#### CRISSCROSS FIRE

*Purpose*: To quickly produce a bed of coals for frying, broiling, toasting, and simmering.

*Method*: Lay a small wigwam fire about six inches high. At the base of this structure place on opposite sides two hard wood sticks about one foot long and two or three inches thick. Upon these foundations build a log cabin around the wigwam, finally laying sticks crisscross over the top. The wood will fall to a bed of coals between the two foundation sticks, which may then be used as a rest for the frying pan. In wet weather lay a small log cabin foundation to raise the wigwam off the ground.

## HUNTER'S FIRE

*Purpose*: To provide a steady fire for cooking several dishes at the same time.

*Method*: Place two green or sound logs six inches apart, or in a V-shape, with the spread ends toward the prevailing wind about seven inches apart, and the other ends about four inches apart. Level off the top of the logs with an ax if you choose. Build either a crisscross fire on top of the logs, to drop down between them when burned to coals, or a fire between the logs with fuzz sticks, kindling, and hard wood sticks. Cooking vessels can span the narrowed end.

## REFLECTOR BAKING FIRE

*Purpose*: To reflect heat into a reflector oven for baking and roasting.

*Method*: Use a large-sized rock for a fireback or construct a fireback by driving two three-foot stakes into the ground, against which you can build up a wall of large sticks or logs, one on top of the other. If neither rocks nor sticks are available, make an earth bank, or use number 10 tins filled with earth. Build a high fire by leaning the sticks against the fireback and place the oven facing it.

## SLEEP

You will be greatly refreshed if you do not sleep in any of the clothing that you have worn during the day, and in warm weather it will be still more agreeable if you can manage to get a quick sponge bath and a rub with a rough towel before you slip into bed. If it is too chilly at night, take a good sponge bath in the morning before you get dressed. A good camper is as scrupulous about personal cleanliness out of doors as she is at home.

When you are snug in your blankets, the excitement and novelty of sleeping in the open may make sleep out of the question at first. Night out of doors is so different from night in a house! A strange feeling of awe overtakes you as you lie drowsily where the stars can look down at you. It is surprising, however, how suddenly sleep comes. You will need a great deal of it after an active day.

### BREAKING CAMP

Okay, the fun's over; time to break camp and head home. Or maybe your luck's still in, and it's only time to move to another site. Either way, the best campers make it their business to *leave no trace* that they were ever there.

- Be sure your fire is out. Burn all charred wood and coals to ash.
- Again, douse your fire completely, stir it thoroughly, and douse again. Then rake out the ash.
- Bury all biodegradable wastes in catholes at least eight inches deep and well away from all water.
- Pack and carry out all packaging, foils, and plastics.
 Make a sport of it. See just how inventive you can be in returning the site to its natural state.

## THE STARS AT NIGHT

So far as there is a central point in our heavens, that point is the Pole-star, Polaris. Around this star all the stars in the sky seem to turn once every twenty-four hours.

Polaris it is easily discovered with the help of the Big Dipper, *a part of the Great Bear*, known to every country boy and girl in the northern half of the world. This is, perhaps, the most important star group in our sky because of its size, peculiar form, the fact that it never sets in our latitude, and that of its stars, two, sometimes called the Pointers, always point out the Pole Star. It is called the Big Dipper because it is shaped like a dipper with a long, bent handle.

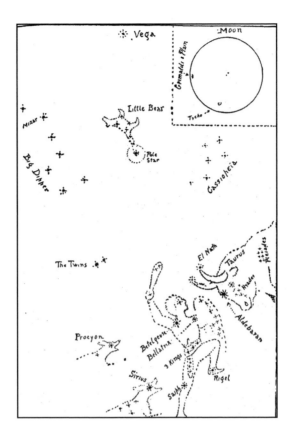

Why the whole group is called the Great Bear is not so easy to explain. The classical legend has it that the nymph, Calisto, having violated her vow, was changed by Diana into a bear, which, after death, was immortalized in the sky by Zeus. Another suggestion is that the earliest astronomers, the Chaldeans, called these stars "the shining ones," and their word happened to be very like the Greek *arktos* (a bear). Another explanation is that vessels in olden days were named for animals. They bore at the prow the carved effigy of the namesake, and if the Great Bear, for example, made several very happy voyages by setting out when a certain constellation was in the ascendant, that constellation might become known as the Great Bear's constellation. Certainly, there is nothing in its shape to justify the name. Very few of the constellations indeed look like the thing they are named after. Their names were usually given for some fanciful association with the namesake, rather than for resemblance to it.

The Pole Star is really the most important of the stars in our sky; it marks the north at all times. All the other stars seem to swing around it once every twenty-four hours. It is in the end of the Little Bear's tail; this constellation is sometimes called the Little Dipper. But the Pole Star, or Polaris, is not a very bright one, and it would be hard to identify but for the help of the Pointers of the Big Dipper.

The outside stars (Alpha and Beta) of the Big Dipper point nearly to Polaris, at a distance equal to five times the space that separates these two stars of the Big Dipper's outer side.

Indian names for the Pole Star are the "Home Star" and "The Star That Never Moves," and they call the Big Dipper the "Broken Back."

The Great Bear is also to be remembered as the hour hand of the woodman's clock. It goes once around the North Star in about twenty-four hours, the same way as the sun, and for the same reason—it is the earth that is going and leaving them behind.

The time in going around is not exactly twenty-four hours, so that the position of the Pointers varies with the seasons, but, as a rule, this is near enough. The bowl of the Big Dipper swings four-fifths of the width of its own opening in one hour. If it went a quarter of the circle, that would mean you had slept a quarter of a day, or six hours.

Every fifteen days the stars seem to be an hour earlier; in three months they gain one-fourth of the circle, and in a year gain the whole circle.

According to Flammarion, there are about seven thousand stars visible to the naked eye, and of these twenty are stars of the first magnitude. Fourteen of them are visible in the latitude of New York, the others belong to the South Polar region of the sky.

## OTHER CONSTELLATIONS

**ORION** (O-ri-on), with its striking array of brilliant stars, Betelgeuze, Rigel, the Three Kings, etc., is generally admitted to be the first constellation in the heavens.

Orion was the hunter giant who went to Heaven when he died and now marches around the great dome. But it is seen only in the winter because, during the summer, he passes over during daytime. Thus he is still the hunter's constellation. The three stars of his belt are called the "Three Kings."

Sirius, the Great Dog star, is in the head of Orion's Hound, the constellation *Canis Major,* and following farther back is the Little Dog star, Procyon, the chief star of the constellation *Canis Minor.*

In old charts of the stars, Orion is shown, with his hounds, hunting the bull, Taurus. This constellation is recognizable by the diagram; the red star, Aldebaran, signals the angry right eye of the Bull. His face is covered with a cluster of little stars called the *Hyades,* and on his shoulder are the seven stars called *Pleiades.*

**PLEIADES** (Ply-a-des) can be seen in winter as a cluster of small stars between Aldebaran and Algol or in a line drawn from the back bottom through the front rim of the Big Dipper, about two Dipper lengths. They are not far from Aldebaran, being in the right shoulder of the Bull. They may be considered the seven arrow wounds made by Orion.

Serviss tells us that the *Pleiades* have a supposed connection with the Great Pyramid, because "about 2170 BC, when the beginning of spring coincided with the culmination of the Pleiades at midnight, that wonderful group of stars was visible just at midnight, through the mysterious southward-pointing passage of the Pyramid."

**CASSIOPEIA** (Cass-e-o-pee-a) is on the opposite side of the Polar Star from the Big Dipper and nearly as far from it. It is a W of five bright stars. This is called *Cassiopeia's Chair.* It is easily found and visible the year round on clear nights.

**THE MOON** is one-fourth the diamenter of the earth, about one-fiftieth of the bulk, and is about a quarter of a million miles away. Its course, while very irregular, is nearly the same as the apparent course of the sun. It is a cold, solid body, without any known atmosphere, and shines by reflected sunlight.

The moon goes around the earth in twenty-seven and a quarter days. It loses about fifty-one minutes in twenty-four hours. Therefore it rises that much later each successive night on average, but there are wide deviations from this average; for example, the time of the Harvest and Hunter's moons in the fall, when the full moon rises at nearly the same time for several nights in succession, denotes from the normal rotation.

According to most authorities, the moon is a piece of the earth that broke away some time ago; and it has followed its mother around ever since.

## THE STARS AS TESTS OF EYESIGHT

In the sky are several tests of eyesight which have been there for some time. The first is the old test of Mizar and Alcor. Mizar, the Horse, is the star at the bend of the handle of the Big Dipper. Just above it is a very small star that astronomers call Alcor, or the rider.

The Indians call these two the "Old Squaw and the Papoose on Her Back." In the old world, from very ancient times, these have been used as tests of eyesight. To be able to see Alcor with the naked eye means that one had excellent eyesight. So also on the plains, the old folks would ask the children at night, "Can you see the papoose on the old Squaw's back?" And when the youngster saw it, and proved that she did by a right description, they rejoiced that she had the eyesight which is the first requisite of a good hunter.

One of the oldest of all eye tests is the Pleiades. Poor eyes see a mere haze, fairly good eyes see five, good eyes see six, and excellent eyes see seven. The rarest eyesight, under the best conditions, see up to ten stars; and, according to Flammarion, the record with unaided eyes is thirteen.

### VEGA OF THE LYRE

If one draws a line from the back wall of the Dipper, that is, from the back bottom star, through the one next to the handle, and continues it upward for twice the total length of the Dipper, it will reach Vega, the brightest star in the northern part of the sky and believed to have been at one time the Pole Star—and likely to be again. Vega, with the two stars near it, form a small triangle. The one on the side next to the North Star is called Epsillon. If you have remarkably good eyes, you will see that it is a double star.

### THE NEBULA IN ORION'S SWORD

Just about in the middle of Orion's Sword is a fuzzy light spot. This might symbolize blood, only it is the wrong color. It is the nebula of Orion. If you can see it with the naked eye, you are to be congratulated.

### ON THE MOON

When the moon is full, there is a large, dark, oval spot on it to the left as you face it, and close to the east rim, almost halfway up; this is the Plain of Grimaldi. It is about twice the size of the whole State of New Jersey, but it is proof of a pair of excellent eyes if you can see it at all.

## A BIRDING WE WILL GO

Preparing for a day of birding includes getting together your bird-watching equipment and properly planning your outing. Usually your day is going to start early, so it is best to prepare the day before.

Your clothing should be comfortable, quiet, and suited to the weather. Almost any casual outdoor wear will be fine. You'll enjoy birding more if your clothing is quiet. Quiet clothing makes it easier for you to hear the wild birds near you. Noisy clothing may even scare off birds and wildlife that are nearby. Bright or shiny clothing should also be avoided, especially anything white. Your clothing does not need to be camouflaged, but it should be neutral in color. Camouflaged clothing has become more popular with birders, but any of the muted earth-tones will work as well.

Weather is always a consideration when selecting clothes for a day of birdwatching. You should be prepared for changes in temperatures and conditions. Dressing in layers is often the best choice. You may want to bring rain gear if rain is in the forecast. A simple lightweight poncho is a good idea in any case.

You won't need much birding equipment, but you will need a pair of binoculars for birding and a field guide at the very least. You may also want to bring along a notebook, pen or pencil, and a camera. For

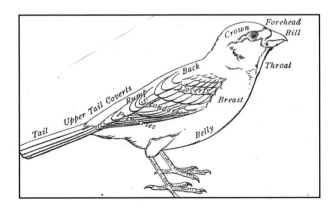

personnel comfort you may want to include sunglasses, insect repellant, cleaning solution for your binoculars, and a water bottle or canteen.

It's a good idea to use a small daypack to carry your birding equipment in. There are also several vests and jackets designed specifically for birders. They typically have multiple pockets to store everything you need.

Prepare a checklist for yourself when planning your first outing. If you realize that you have forgotten something while you are out, make yourself a note to remember it the next time. Taking a little time to prepare will allow you to get the most out of your birding adventure.

## BIRDING ETHICS

Everyone who enjoys birds and birding must always respect wildlife, its environment, and the rights of others. In any conflict of interest between birds and birders, the welfare of the birds and their environment comes first.

### CODE OF BIRDING ETHICS

1. **Promote the welfare of birds and their environment.**
   a. Support the protection of important bird habitat.
   b. To avoid stressing birds or exposing them to danger, exercise restraint and caution during observation, photography, sound recording, or filming.

      Limit the use of recordings and other methods of attracting birds, and never use such methods in heavily birded areas or for attracting any species that is threatened, endangered, of special concern, or is rare in your local area. Keep well back from nests and nesting colonies, roosts, display areas, and important feeding sites. In such sensitive areas, if there is a need for extended observation, photography, filming, or recording, try to use a blind or hide, and take advantage of natural cover.

      Use artificial light sparingly for filming or photography, especially for close-ups.
   c. Before advertising the presence of a rare bird, evaluate the potential for disturbance to the bird, its surroundings, and other people in the area, and proceed only if access can be

controlled, disturbance minimized, and permission has been obtained from private landowners. The sites of rare nesting birds should be divulged only to the proper conservation authorities.

d. Stay on roads, trails, and paths where they exist; otherwise, keep habitat disturbance to a minimum.

2. **Respect the law and the rights of others.**

   a. Do not enter private property without the owner's explicit permission.

   b. Follow all laws, rules, and regulations governing use of roads and public areas, both at home and abroad.

   c. Practice common courtesy in contacts with other people. Your exemplary behavior will generate goodwill with birders and non-birders alike.

3. **Ensure that feeders, nest structures, and other artificial bird environments are safe.**

   a. Keep dispensers, water, and food clean and free of decay or disease. It is important to feed birds continually during harsh weather.

   b. Maintain and clean nest structures regularly.

   c. If you are attracting birds to an area, ensure the birds are not exposed to predation from cats and other domestic animals, or dangers posed by artificial hazards.

4. **Group birding, whether organized or impromptu, requires special care.**

   Each individual in the group, in addition to the obligations spelled out in Items #1 and #2, has responsibilities as a Group Member.

   a. Respect the interests, rights, and skills of fellow birders, as well as people participating in other legitimate outdoor activities. Freely share your knowledge and experience, except where code 1(c) applies. Be especially helpful to beginning birders.

   b. If you witness unethical birding behavior, assess the situation and intervene if you think it prudent. When interceding, inform the person(s) of the inappropriate action and attempt, within reason, to have it stopped. If the behavior continues, document it and notify appropriate individuals or organizations.

Group Leader Responsibilities [amateur and professional trips and tours]:

a. Be an exemplary ethical role model for the group. Teach through word and example.

b. Keep groups to a size that limits impact on the environment and does not interfere with others using the same area.

c. Ensure everyone in the group knows of and practices this code.

d. Learn and inform the group of any special circumstances applicable to the areas being visited (e.g. no tape recorders allowed).

f. Acknowledge that professional tour companies bear a special responsibility to place the welfare of birds and the benefits of public knowledge ahead of the company's commercial interests. Ideally, leaders should keep track of tour sightings, document unusual occurrences, and submit records to appropriate organizations.

## AMERICAN BIRDS

The *bald eagle* is the emblem of America. It is three to four feet from beak to tail, and six or seven feet across the wings. When fully adult it is known by its white head, neck, and tail, and brown body; but when young, it is brownish black, splashed and marked with dull white.

BALD EAGLE

REDTAILED HAWK OR HENHAWK

The only other eagle found in the United States is the *golden,* or *war eagle.* This eagle is a little larger. When full grown it is dark brown, with the basal half of the tail more or less white. The plumage of the young birds is somewhat like that of the young bald eagle; but the two species may always be distinguished by the legs. The war eagle wears leggings—his legs are feathered to the toes. He is ready for the warpath. The bald eagle has the legs bald, or bare, on the lower half.

The *Redtailed hawk,* or *henhawk.* The common hawks of America are very numerous and not easy to distinguish. The best known of the large kinds is the redtail. This is about two feet long and four feet across the wings. In general it is dark brown above and white beneath, with dark brown marks; the tail is clear reddish with one black bar across near the tip. In young birds, the tail is gray with many small bars. It is common in North America east of the Rockies up to mid-Canada. It does much good, killing mice and insects. It is noted for its circling flight and far-reaching whistle or scream.

The *barred,* or *hoot owl* is known at once by the absence of horns, black eyes, and plumage *barred* across the chest and *striped* below. It is about twenty inches long and is generally gray-brown marked with white. It is noted for its loud hooting; it is the noisiest owl in our woods. It is found in the wooded parts of America up to about latitude 50 degrees, east of the Plains.

The *great horned owl,* or *cat owl* is the largest of our owls. About twenty-four inches long and four feet across the wings, it is known at once by its great ear tufts, its yellow eyes, its generally barred plumage of white, black, and buff, and its white front. This is the winged tiger of the woods. Noted for its destruction of game and poultry, it is found throughout the timbered parts of North America.

The *screech owl* is not unlike the horned owl in shape and color but is much smaller—only ten inches long. Sometimes its plumage is red instead of gray. It feeds on mice and insects and has a sweet mournful song in the autumn—its lament for the falling leaves. It is found in the timbered parts of North America.

The *turkey vulture,* or *buzzard* is about two and a half feet long and about six feet across its wings. It is black everywhere except on the under side of the wing, which is gray, and the head, which is naked and red. It is known at once by the naked head and neck and is famous for its splendid flight. It is found from the Atlantic to the Pacific and north to Saskatchewan. It preys on carrion. In the Southern States is another species—the *black vulture*, or *carrion crow*—

(A) BARRED OR HOOT OWL; (B) GREAT HORNED OWL;
(C) TURKEY VULTURE OR BUZZARD; (D) SCREECH OWL

which is somewhat smaller and wears its coat collar up to its ears instead of low on the neck.

The *loon*. The common loon is known by its size—thirty-two inches long and about four feet across the wings—and its brilliant black-and-white plumage. It is noted for its skill as a fisher and diver. Its weird rolling call is heard on every big lake in the country.

LOON AND COMMON SEAGULL

The *common seagull* is twenty-four inches long and four feet across. The plumage is white with a blue-gray back when adult but splashed brown when young, and with black tips to the wings. Its beak is yellow with a red spot on the lower mandible. It is found throughout North America.

The *pelican* is known at once by its great size—about five feet long and eight feet across the wings—by its long beak, by its pouch, and by its fully webbed feet. Its plumage is white but the wing tips are black. It is found in the interior of America.

PELICAN

The *wild duck,* or *mallard,* of all our wild ducks, is the best known. It is about twenty-three inches long. Its bottle-green head, white collar, chestnut breast, penciled sides, and curled-up tail feathers identify it. The female is streaky brown and gray. It is found in all parts of the continent, up to the edge of the forest.

The *wood duck,* or *summer duck* is a beautiful duck about eighteen inches long. Its head is beautifully variegated, bottle-green and white. Its eye is red, its breast a chestnut color, checkered with white spots, while its sides are buff with darker- colored pencilings. This is one of the wildest and

WILD DUCK, OR MALLARD

most beautiful of ducks. It nests in hollow trees and is found in North America up to about latitude 50 degrees.

The *wild goose* is a fine bird about three feet long. Its head and neck are black, its cheek patch white, its body gray, and its tail black with white convert above and below. It is found up to the Arctic regions and breeds in the north at about latitude 45 degrees. It is easily tamed and reared in captivity.

The *bluejay* is a soft purplish blue above and white underneath. The wings and tail are bright blue with black marks. It is found in the woods of America east of the Plains. The bluejay is a wonderful songster and mimic, but it is also mischievous.

The *common crow* is black from head to foot, body and soul. It is about eighteen inches long and thirty wide. It makes itself a nuisance in all the heavily wooded parts of eastern North America.

WOOD DUCK, OR SUMMER
DUCK AND WILD GOOSE,
CANADA GOOSE, OR HONKER

The *bobolink,* or *reedbird* is about seven and a half inches long. The plumage is black and white, with a brown or creamy patch on its nape, and the tail feathers all sharply pointed. The female, and the male in autumn, are all yellow buff with dark streaks. Famous for its wonderful song as it flies over the meadows in June, it is found in North America.

The *baltimore oriole* is about eight inches long, flaming orange in color, with black head and back and partly black tail and wings. The female is duller in plumage. Famous for its beautiful nest, as well as its gorgeous plumage and ringing song, it is abundant in eastern North America in

BLUEJAY AND BOBOLINK, OR REEDBIRD

open woods up to northern
Ontario and Lake Winnipeg.

The *purple grackle,* or *crow
blackbird* is the northern bird
of paradise that looks black at
a distance but its head is shiny
blue and its body iridescent. It
is twelve inches long. When flying it holds its long tail with the
edge raised like a boat, hence
"boat tail." In various forms it

BALTIMORE ORIOLE AND PURPLE GRACKLE,
OR CROW BLACKBIRD

COMMON HOUSE WREN AND
CHICKADEE

ROBIN

is found throughout the eastern States and in Canada up to Hudson
Bay.

The *common house wren* is about five inches long; soft brown above
and brownish gray below, it is barred with dusky brown on wings and
tail. It nests in a hole and is found in wooded America east of the Plains
and north to Saskatchewan, Ottawa, and Maine.

The *chickadee* is a cheerful little bird five and a half inches long. Its
cap and throat are black. Its upper parts are gray, its under parts brownish, its cheeks white, and there are no streaks anywhere. It does not
migrate, so it is well known in the winter woods of eastern America up

BLUEBIRD

WOOD THRUSH

to the Canadian region where the brown-capped, or Hudson chickadee takes its place.

The *robin* is about ten inches long, mostly dark gray in color, but with black on head and tail; its breast is brownish red. The spots about the eye, also the throat, the belly, and the marks in outer tail feathers are white. Its mud nest is known in nearly every orchard. The robin is found throughout the timbered parts of America north to the limit of trees.

The *wood thrush* is about eight inches long, cinnamon-brown above, brightest on the head, white below, and with black spots on breast and sides. The wood thrush is distinguished from the many thrushes in America, much like it, by the reddish head and round black spots on its under sides. It is found in the woods of eastern North America up to Vermont and Minnesota.

The *bluebird* is about seven inches long, brilliant blue above, dull red-brown on breast, and white below. It's found in eastern North America, north to about latitude 50 degrees in the interior and not so far on the coast.

## BIRD NOTES

*By Celia Thaxter*

### FOOD OF BIRDS

By carpentering, by painting, by selling goods—by so many different kinds of work that it would be hard to make a list of them all—your fathers provide your daily food.

Long ago, in the old forests of England or Germany, our ancestors got their own food by hunting, fishing, keeping cattle, and by a little farming. Today this work is done for us, but the birds still have to do their foraging for themselves.

Birds eat the things which you eat, and besides have the whole insect world to hunt in. You can often tell by a bird's appearance what she eats, and when you have found that out, you can generally tell where she will choose to live, and what many of her habits of life are. When you see the wide mouth of a swallow, and her long, slender wings, you will decide that if any bird could catch the hosts of flies, gnats, and beetles that fill the air in summer, certainly the swallow should be well fitted for such hunting. When you remember that hard frosts kill these flying insects, you will feel sure that you will find no swallows here in winter. The long, sharp bill of a heron, and her long, naked feet seem well fitted for spearing frogs finds the insects she has learned to catch. Sometimes a bird's food depends so largely on a certain tree that she will have to leave a town, if these trees are all cut down.

Sometimes birds have found a certain kind of food or a way of getting food so different from that of any other bird that their bills or feet have gradually changed, and they have become more and more dependent on this way of getting their living. The woodpecker's tongue is a long, hooked brush, with which she rakes out grubs from deep holes, the humming bird's tongue is a tube through which she sucks honey, and the flamingo's bill is a sieve through which she strains muddy water as a whale strains the sea water through her whalebone meshes.

You could find many stories about the strange food or feeding habits of birds. First, however, look about you, if you can, and find out what the birds that are your own neighbors eat and how they get it. Take the common birds, the robin, the chipping sparrow, the kingbird, and the gull, and watch them till you see them getting and eating their dinner. Then you will be all the more interested in the interesting stories you will find in the books. You will learn, too, what patience and sharp sight people come to have who watch birds and find out all their secrets.

When their feathers drop out, others grow out to take their places, and in a month or so the bird has a new suit of fine strong feathers, all ready to carry her to her distant winter home.

With many of the birds of the duck and goose family, the moulting goes so quickly that the bird has scarcely enough feathers to enable her to fly. She hides during these unhappy weeks in distant swamps, hoping that no enemy will attack her till she is ready to fly again. She must feel like a cripple and try her wings impatiently, longing for the day when she can be off again through the air.

In the case of many gay-colored male birds, this summer moult leaves them very shabby-looking. The Bobolink loses all his gay black and white, and comes out in August in brown and yellow, like his wife and children. He probably does not feel so proud of his good looks as before, but I think he is safer. The black and white was so bright that his enemies could easily see him, but now he can slip away among the brown grasses and hardly be noticed.

Many male birds are not content with one suit of feathers a year. They have to have another new suit, or part of one, in the spring, and of the gayest colors and feathers. Red and blue and yellow appear on the shoulders, in the tail, on the head, neck, and breast, in patches, bars, bands, and streaks.

## HOW YOUNG BIRDS GET FED

One afternoon in July, I watched six little Barn Swallows sitting on the roof of a barn. They had evidently left their nest only a few days before, but their wings were already strong enough to carry them back to the roof if they fluttered off.

Soon the father approached and was greeted by six gaping mouths. The little bird sitting nearest him got the mouthful, and an instant later got another from the mother. Six times in succession she was fed, neither parent regarding the five other yellow throats.

This seemed unfair and foolish as well. I thought little birds must be starved one day and fed too full the next. I waited a few moments and the mystery was solved. The little bird who had been getting so much soon had all she wanted. The next time the parents came her mouth was shut, and one of the other five got the mouthful.

When a cat or a dog has had enough, she stops eating. It must be so with little birds too; when one has had enough, she shuts her mouth and eyes and dozes while her brothers and sisters get their meal. I fear, though, that when there are six mouths to fill, the last is hardly closed before the first opens again.

BLACK-THROATED GREEN WARBLERS

Herons live and fish in shallow water. They must therefore live near water and in winter go where the swamps are not frozen.

Such birds, as crows, eat many kinds of food; whatever they can get, in fact. In spring the farmer's corn tastes sweet to them, but the grubs and beetles are good food, too, and they find that no one will shoot them for taking the grubs, while eating corn means taking some risk. In fall and winter, nuts are also added to the crow's bill of fare. Near the seashore, dead fish and other sea animals which are found on the shore vary the food in winter. I am ashamed to say that eggs, and even young birds, are sometimes devoured by the crow. When a bird is so easily pleased, and has such a wide choice, she can stay all the year round.

Seed-eating birds, like the sparrows, can find seeds on the weeds and grasses even in winter, and the little bark inspectors find eggs, cocoons, and sleepy beetles in the cracks of the bark, so that winter does not frighten them away. Many of the sea birds, especially the divers, can find fish or shellfish in the winter sea, where it does not freeze over.

## WHEN A BIRD CHANGES HER CLOTHES

Do you know how important the masts of a sailing ship are? If they are broken, the ship is helpless. It drifts about wherever the wind blows it.

A bird's wing and tail feathers are as important for its safety as the mast and sails of a ship. The strong, powerful quill feathers enable it to fly rapidly through the air to get its food and to avoid its enemies. It is important that the feathers of both wings should be uninjured, for the bird would be unable to guide its flight if one wing were much less strong than the other.

Feathers get worn by use, some even get broken, and if the bird could not replace them it would have hard work, after a year or two, to make the old, weatherworn ones do their work.

Nature, however, provides the birds with a new suit of clothes every year. After the young are hatched, when the old birds no longer need their swiftness and strength to get the daily food for their children, the feathers of almost all birds begin to drop out; not at once, for that would leave the bird naked and helpless, but gradually and, in the case of the wing feathers, fairly evenly—as fast a way that can make the bird attractive. The little fellows know very well what a fine appearance they now make. If there is any bit of color that does not show well, they take pains to bow or bend, or to spread wing or tail to display it. All these bright feathers are moulted again and the winter suit put on. So the suits change with the seasons, till the little life is ended.

The humming birds are a perpetual pleasure. I shall never forget the surprise of joy the first time one alighted on my sleeve and rested, as much at home as if I were a stick or harmless twig.

Sparrows and Nuthatches had often alighted on my head as I stood musing over my flowers, but to have this tiny spark of brilliant life come to anchor, as it were, on anything so earthly as my arm was indeed a nine days' wonder. Now it has grown to be an old story, but it is never any less delightful.

# GOTTA DANCE

## BALLET

The thing we call "Classical Ballet" got its start nearly 500 years ago in the France of Louis XIII and Louis XIV. Traditionally, men danced all the roles. It was not until quite a few years later that women were permitted to dance on the stage. Many of the best-known ballets are taken from folk and fairy tales. Many come also from bible stories, historical events, and popular legends.

### BASIC CLASSICAL BALLET POSITIONS

#### *FIRST POSITION*

Your back is straight, your weight is evenly distributed on both legs, your heels are touching, and your feet are in full turn-out, forming a straight line. Your hands are held in front of you at waist level.

#### *SECOND POSITION*

Place your feet fully turned out as in first position, except that here your feet are about one foot apart. Again keep your back straight and your weight evenly distributed on both legs. Raise your arms out and to the sides until they are angled slightly downward. Hold the palms of your hand facing downwards.

#### *THIRD POSITION*

Your feet remain fully turned out as in first and second positions. Again, keep your back straight and you attention to the front. Cross one foot until it is halfway in front of the other. Hold one arm as in first position, the other as in second position.

#### *FOURTH POSITION*

With your feet still turned out, bring one foot in front of the other so that your toes and your heels are in line with one another. In this position there ought to be a distance of eight or nine inches between your feet. As you move to this position from third position, sweep your lower arm up into a curve above your head. Again, keep your back straight and your attention to the front.

## FIFTH POSITION

Bring one foot exactly in front of the other. This is the same stance as in forth position except that now your feet are touching. As you take this position, bring both arms up above your head into a curve. Again, keep your back straight, shoulders squared, and attention toward the front.

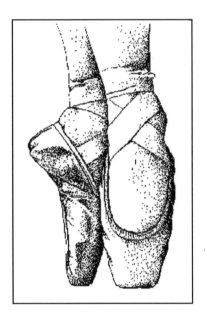

BASIC CLASSICAL BALLET

## THE DEMI-PLIE

This is a half-bend of the knees in two counts. Hold your back and shoulders straight and to the front, facing the barre. Practice in each of the five basic positions.

## THE GRAND PLIE

This is a full bend of the knees in four counts going down and four counts coming up. Your heels lift in the downward bend (except in second position) then push down while passing through demi-plie to standing position. Practice in each of the five basic positions.

## BATTEMENTS TENDUS

While centering your weight over the ball of your foot, bring your leg and foot out and back in a controlled slide as you move it from the front, to the side, and to the back.

## BATTEMENTS DEGAGES

This is much the same as in *Battements Tendus* except that as you point your foot, you raise it three inches or so above the floor. This step is executed in four counts, ending in the position it began in at count four.

## RONDS DE JAMBE A TERRE

Here the toes point to the floor as the dancer slides her foot to the front, then (continuing to point) around to the side (as in second position), then to the back, and finishing in first position.

## GLISSADES

These are gliding steps that are most often used to link other steps together.

In French, the word "ballet" means simply "dance." And it is in this simple sense of the word that we can best understand ballet in its universality—that every dance is a ballet.

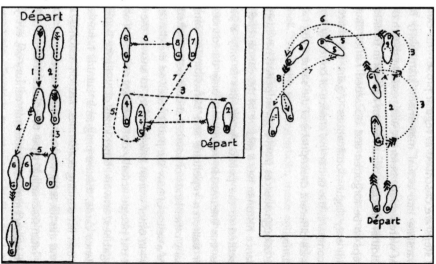

## TAP

Tap dancing is drumming with your feet. It takes its origins from the folk jigs, clog hops, and step dancing of the old days. Mix the rhythms of the African drums with the syncopation of jazz, and a little bit of blues, and you begin to understand where this music of the feet comes from.

A lot of tap dancers were, and are still, called "hoofers."

The basics of tap dancing are easily learned, if not mastered, in pretty quick order if you work at it. Tap dancing is not only great exercise but it's about the most fun a person can have dancing.

---

### BASIC TAP

#### FLAP

You shift your weight to one foot, brush the other foot forward, and put the ball of your foot down. You can do this backwards and forwards and off to the side.

#### SHUFFLE

Standing on one foot, you brush the other foot backwards and forwards.

#### BALL CHANGE

You shift your weight from one foot to the other.

#### FLAP BALL CHANGE

You brush your right foot forward, shift your weight to that right foot, and take two steps; then you do the same on left side.

#### SHUFFLE BALL CHANGE

With your weight on your left foot, brush your right foot forward and then back again, then take two steps (right, left).

## TANGO

The middle to late 19th century saw a flood of immigrants (primarily from Spain and Italy) from all over Europe wash up on the shores of South America. There they mixed together, in the cities of Buenos Aries and Montevideo particularly. They brought with them the music and dance of the old country, their waltzes, polkas, and mazurkas; and their instruments too: their violins, flutes, clarinets, flamingo guitars and bandoneons (accordion-like instruments). In very short order these had mixed with the folk music of Argentina and other native song and dance of South America, with the rhythms of African slave song and with the Cuban habanera.

It was from this rich stew of cultures, dance, and music that tango was born.

### SAMPLE TANGOS

The following three samples represent a veritable menu of tango steps and routines.

Of course this is nothing like all the possibilities—they number in the hundreds and hundreds—but it is a start. Why not begin by choosing a step here, a routine there, and creating your very own tango?

### *TANGO 1*

#### Tango Walk

In promenade position, the woman walks six steps forward, turning a half turn on count six, and continuing two more steps in line of direction on the inside of the circle. The man walks two steps forward. On the third step, he turns in front of the woman and walks backward on counts four and five. On count six, the couple turns with the man walking forward (the couple walks forward around each other as in a Pomander turn) and turns into his original position, while the woman walks forward and pivots slightly to resume promenade position.

---

### GRAPEVINE

Moving to the right, you step out on your right foot, cross your left foot behind, step out on your right foot, and cross your left foot in front. Moving to the left, you step out on your left foot, cross your right foot behind, step out on your left foot, and cross your right foot in front.

---

### Drag and Pivot

With the man facing out and the woman facing in, each steps side to side (toward the line of direction) with their first feet and drag the second feet to close. Repeat on counts three and four. End with four pivots.

### Grape Vine with Dip

This is an alternating grapevine. On count seven, bend the second knee, pointing the first foot in line of direction. On count eight, close the first foot to the second.

### Half Grape Vine, Dip, and Pivot

Backing the woman, the man takes one step forward right then takes one step forward left, crossing in front of the right. Bend the right knee, extending the left foot to the side. On count four, straighten the knee and close the feet together.

---

### BRIEF GLOSSARY OF TANGO TERMS

*Line of Direction* (also called *Line of Dance*): The direction in which all couples move around the dance floor, most often counterclockwise.

*Ballroom Position*: Partners are face-to-face, most often backing the woman in the man's line of direction, his right arm around her waist, her left hand on his shoulder, and his left hand holding her right hand a little out and to the side.

*Promenade Position*: Both partners face forward in line of direction; they stand side by side, most often holding hands as in ballroom position.

*Over-the-Shoulders Position*: This is a reverse promenade in which the handholds are the same but the partners are looking away (the man looks over his right shoulder and the woman looks over her left).

*The First Foot*: In Tango, most often the woman's left foot and the man's right foot are considered first feet, the opposite foot being the second foot. In nearly all promenade and ballroom steps, partners begin on opposite feet.

*The Grapevine*: This is basically a series of side cross steps, alternating with the active foot crossing in front of and behind the pivot foot.

*The Media Luna*: This is essentially a box step: right foot one step forward, left foot one step crossing forward and to the right of the right foot, the right foot then steps back to original position, followed by the left foot also to starting position.

*The Scissors*: From a promenade walk, the partners turn to face one and other, stepping across their own feet, and twisting back and forth.

## TANGO 2

### Position and Two-Step

Backing the woman, each dancer takes one small step in the line of direction. On count two, point the second foot to the side, looking over the shoulders at the pointed foot. On counts three and four, do one two-step in the line of direction. Repeat.

### Dip, Two-Step, Walk, and Circle Foot

In promenade position, step forward on the first foot and dip forward, bending the leading knee. Two-step forward on the inner foot, walk forward two steps (first foot, second foot), and swing first (outside) foot in *media luna* to meet partner's foot with toes pointed to the floor.

Double Scissors

With the man starting left and the woman right, both do crossing scissors with points: cross first foot, cross second, cross first, point first to the side. *(Scissors are usually done with partners facing one another.)*

## *TANGO 3*

### The Tango Two-Step

Partners hold hands in open position (the woman on the man's right side). The couple walks forward two steps, each starting on his or her own first foot, then close feet on count three, bend, and pivot slightly away from his or her partner. Repeat on opposite feet, facing your partner (four, five, and six) and on counts seven and eight, the woman steps around to ballroom position.

Dip and Two-Step as in Tango 2. Repeat.

Four two-steps: Backing the woman, turning backing the man *(who also turns)*. Backing the man, the woman dips forward on her right knee and the man dips back on his left foot. Then, do one two-step forward. Repeat. Then do thirty-two bars of ordinary turning two-steps.

# LIFESTYLE

## GREAT AMERICAN WOMEN

1. **Abigail Adams:** U.S. First Lady and wife of former U.S. President John Adams who modeled an expanded role for women in public affairs during the formative days of the United States.
2. **Madeleine Albright:** First woman to become U.S. Secretary of State.
3. **Louisa May Alcott:** Novelist best known for writing *Little Women*, published in 1868.
4. **Maya Angelou:** American autobiographer and poet, and one of the first African-American women able to publicly discuss her personal life.
5. **Susan B. Anthony:** Civil rights leader who played a key role in the 19th-century women's rights movement to introduce women's suffrage in the United States.
6. **Lucille Ball:** Comedian, film executive, and film, television, stage, and radio actress who, with thirty years under her belt, had one of Hollywood's longest careers. She received thirteen Emmy Award nominations and had four wins.
7. **Clara Barton:** Teacher, nurse, and humanitarian best remembered for organizing the American Red Cross.
8. **Elizabeth Blackwell:** First U.S. female doctor and the first woman to graduate from medical school who was a pioneer in educating women in medicine.
9. **Willa Cather:** Author best-known for her depictions of frontier life on the Great Plains.
10. **Sandra Day O'Connor:** First female Justice of the U.S. Supreme Court.
11. **Emily Dickinson:** Poet whose poems are unique for the era in which she wrote—many dealing with themes of death and immortality.
12. **Amelia Earhart:** Aviation pioneer, author, and the first woman to fly solo across the Atlantic Ocean.
13. **Ella Fitzgerald:** One of the most influential jazz vocalists of the 20th century.
14. **Betty Friedan:** Feminist activist, primary founder of the National Organization for Women, and a writer best-known for starting

the "second wave of the Women's Movement" with her book *The Feminine Mystique.*

15. **Ruth Bader Ginsburg:** Associate Justice on the U.S. Supreme Court and the first Jewish woman to serve in that capacity.

16. **Katharine Hepburn:** Actress who holds the record for the most Best Actress Oscar wins with four, from twelve nominations, during her seventy three-year career. In 1999, the American Film Institute ranked her as the greatest female star in the history of American cinema.

17. **Zora Neale Hurston:** Folklorist and author during the Harlem Renaissance best-known for writing the novel *Their Eyes Were Watching God.*

18. **Mahalia Jackson:** African-American gospel singer with a powerful, distinct voice who is widely regarded as one of the most influential gospel singers in the world. She was dubbed the first "Queen of Gospel Music."

19. **Jackie Joyner-Kersee:** Ranked among the all-time greatest athletes in the women's heptathlon and women's long-jump who won three gold, one silver, and two bronze medals over four consecutive Olympic Games.

20. **Helen Keller:** Author, political activist, and lecturer who was the first deaf-blind person to earn a Bachelor of Arts degree.

21. **Billie Jean King:** Tennis player who won twelve Grand Slam singles titles, sixteen Grand Slam women's doubles titles, and eleven Grand Slam mixed doubles titles, and advocate against sexism in sports and society.

22. **Dorothea Lange:** Documentary photographer and photojournalist best known for her photographs that humanized the tragic consequences of the Great Depression.

23. **Maya Y. Lin:** Architectural designer and sculptor who at twenty-one years old won the design competition for the Vietnam Veterans War Memorial, which has since become the most-visited monument in Washington, D.C. and one of the most well-known memorials in the world.

24. **Madonna:** Recording artist, actress, and entrepreneur ranked by the Recording Industry Association of America as the best-selling female rock artist of the 20th century and named world's most successful female recording artist of all time by the Guinness Book of Records in 2007.

25. **Margaret Mead:** Cultural anthropologist who contributed to the development of the discipline while introducing its insights to people outside the academy.
26. **Florence Nightingale:** Pioneering nurse, writer, and noted statistician considered to be the founder of modern nursing.
27. **Annie Oakley:** Exhibition sharpshooter whose talent and timely rise to fame led to a starring role in Buffalo Bill's Wild West Show, propelling her to become the first American female superstar.
28. **Rosa Parks:** African-American civil rights activist whom the U.S. Congress later called the "Mother of the Modern-Day Civil Rights Movement."
29. **Janet Reno:** First female U.S. Attorney General whose tenure was the second-longest in history.
30. **Sally Ride:** Physicist and former NASA astronaut who, in 1983, became the first American woman and youngest at the time, to fly into space.
31. **Eleanor Roosevelt:** U.S. First Lady and advocate for civil rights who continued to be an internationally-prominent author, speaker, politician, and activist for the New Deal coalition even after the death of her husband, former President Franklin D. Roosevelt.
32. **Sacagawea:** A Shoshone woman who accompanied the Lewis and Clark Expedition in their exploration of the Western United States.
33. **Bessie Smith:** American blues singer of the 1920s and 1930s who was often regarded as one of the greatest singers of her era.
34. **Margaret Chase Smith:** Longest-serving female senator in U.S. history, and the first woman to be elected to both the U.S. House and U.S. Senate. She was also the first woman to have her name placed in nomination for the U.S. Presidency at a major party's convention—the 1964 Republican Convention.
35. **Harriet Beecher Stowe:** American abolitionist and author whose novel, *Uncle Tom's Cabin*, helped bring the nation's attention to the horrors of slavery.
36. **Gloria Steinem:** Feminist icon, journalist, and social and political activist who was a founder of *New York* magazine and one of the most important heads of the Woman's Rights Movement.
37. **Sojourner Truth:** Abolitionist and women's rights activist who was born into slavery; best known for her speech "Ain't I a Woman?"

38. **Harriet Tubman:** African-American abolitionist, humanitarian, and Union spy during the American Civil War who escaped from slavery and made thirteen missions via the Underground Railroad to rescue more than seventy slaves.

39. **Oprah Winfrey:** Media mogul and philanthropist whose internationally-syndicated talk show, *The Oprah Winfrey Show*, is the highest-rated talk show in the history of television and has earned her multiple Emmy Awards.

40. **Mildred "Babe" Didrikson Zaharias:** Athlete who achieved outstanding success in golf, basketball, and track and field whom the Associated Press voted as the Greatest Female Athlete of the first half of the 20th century.

## BEAUTY TIPS

*By Lara L. Brennan*

Of course the best way to health and beauty is through a good diet and plenty of exercise.

To avoid pimples and blemishes, wash your hands and face regularly. As simple as this may sound, it is the best way to avoid breakouts. Once you start to get older, your face becomes oily and these oils on your face are most often the cause of blemishes.

Wash your hands! One way those oils get on your face is by touching your face with your hands.

If you have frizzy hair, there are many things that you can do to keep your hair manageable. After shampooing, try conditioning your hair. Leave the conditioner in for a few minutes before washing it out, and after you get out of the shower, wrap up your hair in a towel and let it dry there. If you have dull, lifeless hair, wash it often and condition. Avoid too much use of the curling (or straightening) iron, as the heat will damage your hair over time.

Do you ever get bags under your eyes? I know I have and wished that there was some way to get rid of them. But the first step in getting rid of unsightly bags is learning what causes them. Now, if you are like I was, you probably think that the reason for the bags under your eyes is mostly due to lack of sleep. And as you grow older, and your bedtime is pushed back later and later, this theory probably makes pretty good sense to you. However, there may be other causes, like a poor diet or even heredity causes. Some people say that you get bags under your eyes from eating too much salty food. Too bad, I love salty food.

Many people say that putting wet tea bags on your closed lids will work wonders. But really, any damp, cool compress will do the trick.

Don't leave make-up on overnight.

The old expression goes that beauty is only skin-deep. But don't you believe it. Every person has a part of her that is beautiful. Your goal should be to discover what is beautiful in yourself and work to bring it out. This may be the best beauty tip of all.

## YOGA

People used to believe that yoga was only stretching exercises, mantra repetition, and breathing techniques. But this is not entirely true. The whole point of yoga, throughout its 5000 year history, has been to teach one to cope with the many physical, psychological, and spiritual trials in life. You can best hope to achieve good health and happiness only if all the areas of your life are in balance. Practicing yoga teaches you to create a balance between your mind, body, and soul. With balance you may achieve a calm, focused mind and a strong, flexible body; also you'll have a sense of unity, harmony, and satisfaction—in short, *peace of mind*.

Yoga is one of the six great schools of Indian thought, together called the *darsana*, or *the way to see*. Yoga can be best described as a metaphysical way to clarity of mind and good health. Yoga is not a religion; instead, it is connected to the philosophical traditions of India.

Yoga can be compared to a tree on which each single branch represents a certain movement or path. The most famous branches are *Tantra Yoga* (this is the oldest branch, "the main trunk"), *Bhakti Yoga* (devotion), *Jnana Yoga* (knowledge/wisdom), *Raja Yoga* (meditation/introspection), *Karma Yoga* (action), and *Hatha Yoga* (forceful physical yoga).

**Tantra Yoga** is the oldest path in yoga. Through tantric techniques, you can gradually learn to sense, understand, and see energy. This path works with the symbolic energy *shakti* (feminine energy) in order to evoke the *Kundalini*-power (the primordial power) that is located at the bottom of the spine. Tantra Yoga embraces all other paths in yoga.

It sometimes uses the body to carry out different exercises and meditations. The purpose is to promote positive thoughts and become more conscious of sexual energy.

*Bhakti Yoga.* Bhakti means emotional devotion towards the divine. Bhakti Yoga is the path of love and devotion. This devotion is expressed in prayers, rituals, and ceremonial worshipping. You give praise to the divine in all of nature's creatures. This type of yoga focuses on worshipping the divinity you find in your own heart and mind.

*Jnana Yoga.* Jnana means wisdom and knowledge. This is the intellectual path in yoga. The goal here is to achieve a pure mind freed from shallowness and vanity. In Jnana Yoga, you create balance through trying to separate reality from illusion (*maya*) so that you can achieve clarity and strength.

*Raja Yoga.* Raja Yoga combines all branches of yoga, and it can include Karma, Jnana, and Bhakti. Raja means "royal," and Raja Yoga sees the body as a "vehicle" for spiritual energy. Raja Yoga primarily focuses on meditation and on consciously controlling the human mind. Raja Yoga arose due to the work of Patanjali and the text *Yoga Sutras.*

*Karma Yoga.* Karma means action. This branch of yoga works on achieving balance through unselfish actions (primarily through some sort of community service). Karma is suitable for people who have a calm and patient nature and who are interested in supporting and working with other people.

*Hatha Yoga* is often called "the path of the body" or "classical yoga." Hatha Yoga is a sequence of *asanas,* or poses, that train the body, soul, and mind. Hatha means "power" and "strength."

## BOOKS FOR ADVENTUROUS GIRLS

*Little Dorrit* by Charles Dickens
*Heidi* by Johanna Spyri
*Wuthering Heights* by Charlotte Bronte
*To Kill a Mockingbird* by Harper Lee
*The Diary of Anne Frank*
*Pride And Prejudice* by Jane Austen
*Anna and the King of Siam* by Margaret Landon

*Wolf by the Ears* by Ann Rinaldi
*A Break with Charity* by Ann Rinaldi
*Finishing Becca* by Ann Rinaldi
*The Coffin Quilt* by Ann Rinaldi
*The Story of the Trapp Family Singers* by Maria von Trapp
*I Capture the Castle* by Dodie Smith
*Silas Marner* by George Eliot
*Gigi* by Colette
*The Giggler Treatment* by Roddy Doyle
*Lily's Crossing* by Patricia Reilly Giff
*Monkey Town* by Ronald Kidd
*Witch Hunt* by Mark Aaronson
*January 1905* by Katharine Boling
*Black Beauty* by Anna Sewell
*My Friend Flicka* by Mary O'Hara
*Ashes of Roses* by M. J. Auch
*The Phantom Tollbooth* by Norton Juster and Jules Feiffer
*From the Mixed-up Files of Mrs. Basil E. Frankweiler* by E. L. Konigsburg
*The Clique* by Lisi Harrison
*Kiki Strike* by Kristen Miller
*The Westing Game* by Ellen Raskin
*The Stolen Sapphire* by Sarah Masters Buckley
*Kira-Kira* by Cynthia Kadohata
*A Tree Grows in Brooklyn* by Betty Smith
*Gilda Joyce, Psychic Investigator* by Jennifer Allison
*The True Confessions of Charlotte Doyle* by Avi
*I'd Tell You I Love You But then I'd Have to Kill You* by Ally Carter
*The Princess Bride* by William Goldman
*Home: A Memoir of My Early Years* by Julie Andrews

## SERIES

*Harry Potter* by J. K. Rowling
*Twilight* by Stephenie Meyer
*Nancy Drew* by Carolyn Keen
*The Chronicles of Narnia* by C. S. Lewis
Jacky Faber Adventures

## ABBREVIATIONS FOR EMAIL AND TEXTING

| | |
|---|---|
| aml | all my love |
| asap | as soon as possible |
| b4 | before |
| b4n | bye for now |
| bbl | be back later |
| bf | best friend |
| bff | best friend forever |
| brb | be right back |
| cul8ter | see you later |
| fyeo | for your eyes only |
| fyi | for your information |
| g2g | got to go |
| gb | good bye |
| gl | good luck |
| gr8 | great |
| ic | I see |
| idk | I don't know |
| ik | I know |
| jk | just kidding |
| lol | laugh out loud |
| nbd | no big deal |
| nfn | not found in nature |
| pcm | please call me |
| pu! | what a stink! |
| r | are |
| ruok? | are you ok? |
| sry | sorry |
| thx | thanks |
| u | you |
| wkd | weekend |
| x | kiss |

# OTHER THINGS AN ADVENTUROUS
# GIRL SHOULD KNOW

## HOW TO SAVE A LIFE

"First Aid" is emergency treatment until a physician can arrive. Exact knowledge of First Aid may save human life.

General Directions:

**Be Calm!** Stay Cool. **Think!** See what is wrong.

### WHAT TO DO

Send for a doctor if the accident is at all serious.

Keep the patient comfortable. Reassure her. Keep any crowd away. Be careful about moving her. Cover her if she's cold. Make her head comfortable. Relieve any pain wherever you can. If she vomits, turn her head to one side (preferably the right side), so her mouth can drain. Do not do too much beyond this.

### SEE WHAT FIRST AID IS NEEDED (IF ANY)

Look for spurting blood or heavy bleeding and relieve it with a sterile compress bandaged firmly on the wound or by pressing your finger on the skin over the blood vessel at the location of the pressure point, or very carefully by tourniquet if necessary.

### *LOOK FOR BREATHING AND COVER WOUNDS*

Be sure nothing tight interferes with breathing.

Cover all wounds with a sterile compress and bandage. The fingers should not touch a wound. Never cover a wound with a dirty dressing.

### *LOOK FOR FRACTURES*

Don't move the patient until splints have been applied.

### *LOOK AT THE FACE*

If it's flushed, the patient should recline with feet slightly lower than the head; if the face is pale, recline with head slightly lower than the feet.

## LOOK FOR SHOCK

Shock usually follows an injury. To relieve it, lower the head of the patient and apply blankets to keep the patient warm. A warm drink, such as tea, is also a good idea. The point is to warm the patient both inside and outside.

If you know the patient has taken poison, try to induce vomiting.

Be careful of moving the patient until you are certain that no bones are broken—a simple fracture may become a compound if jostled! Also there may be internal injuries which moving may aggravate.

Wounds without severe bleeding constitute the majority of all wounds. For small wounds, it is desirable to encourage enough bleeding to clean the wound before dressing. Or even better, clean the wound with soap and warm water, then apply antiseptic before bandaging. The pressure of a compress (pad) under a bandage will stop most bleeding if firmly held or firmly bound into place.

## WOUNDS BLEEDING FREELY

Bleeding may be **arterial**—out of the arteries which carry the blood from the heart. Nature protects these by putting them deep on the inside of limbs. If an artery is cut, the bleeding must be quickly stopped or else the spurting may quickly cause the victim to bleed to death.

**Venous** bleeding is from the veins which carry the blood back to the heart and is a relatively smoother flow.

**Capillary** bleeding is the slow oozing from the very fine blood vessels.

All three may be going on at once.

The treatment for bleeding is to save loss of blood and check the bleeding so that nature can close up the broken vessels with blood clots. The "pressure points" where the flow can be cut off are therefore very important. Thus the flow can be reduced until a bandage compress can be placed.

## STOPPING BLEEDING BY PRESSURE

Know *where* to stop severe bleeding. There are three main pipelines running from the pumping station, known as the heart—three on the right side and of course three to supply the left side.

One goes up to the head.

One goes out to each arm.

One goes down to each leg.

### THE HEAD

- Neck—shuts off entire head on that side.
- Angle of Jaw—shuts off lower half of jaw.
- Temple—shuts off upper half of head. (See No. 1.)

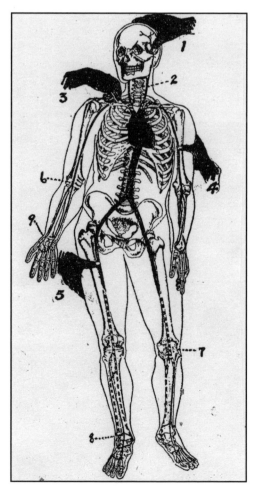

DOTTED LINES INDICATE THAT THE ARTERIES LIE
ON THE BACK SIDE

### THE ARM

- Back of collar bone
- Under arm (Pad with arm pressure)
- Inner side of upper arm
- Bend of elbow (Bent tightly)
- Wrist
- Base of thumb
- Base of little finger
- Palm of hand (Gripping on any pad)

### THE LEG

These shut off everything below the pressure point involved:
- Upper thigh
- Bend of knee (Back side—in the bend)
- Inner ankle (Back of ankle bone)
- Outer ankle (Front of ankle bone)
- Sole of foot (Push pad with foot against something solid)

### FIRST AID

Stop the flow! You can do so by:
1) a sterile compress pressed firmly on the wound.
2) hand pressure on the part affected using your knowledge of pressure points.

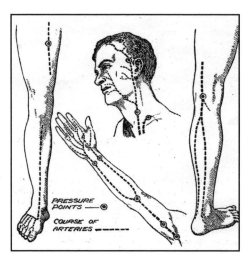

PRESSURE POINTS —●

COURSE OF ARTERIES - - - - -

Elevate the wounded part above the body level if possible.

If bleeding still persists, tie a square knot in a handkerchief loosely around the limb affected then insert your hand upside down close to and above the wound, and tighten by twisting your hand. [A stick may be used to tighten but it can easily be made so tight as to be injurious. This is less likely with the hand.]

If blood flow is thus cut off, be sure to loosen the hold every fifteen or twenty minutes or else the limb may be permanently injured. A clot should form in about ten minutes unless the wound is extremely large.

With severe bleeding keep the patient quiet and lying on her back. She will be thirsty—she may have cold water in small quantities.

The patient is also likely to go into shock.

## FAINTING

### *DEFINITION*

Fainting is extreme weakness or unconsciousness due to stoppage of blood supply to the brain.

### *SYMPTOMS*

Dizziness and unsteadiness on the feet or unconsciousness and falling down. The fall is the chief danger in fainting. When someone is feeling faint, the face is pale, the pulse weak and rapid, there's a cold sweat, and breathing is shallow and irregular. If they fall, let them lie still and make sure they are all right.

### *FIRST AID*

First, give the patient some air—fainting usually occurs in overcrowded, overheated places, so lay the patient down with her head lower than the rest of her body so blood will flow to the head. Keep her warm—if necessary, a little cold water may be sprinkled on her face.

Never try to give a stimulant to an unconscious person. Let the patient rest—do not hurry her. Keep her warm. She should avoid needless physical exertion.

If you feel yourself fainting, the following measures are preventative:

If *sitting*—lean forward, placing your head between your knees.
If *standing*—place your arm tightly against your chest, pull in, then push out your diaphragm. The idea is to force blood to your head.

## SHOCK

### DEFINITION

Shock is a nervous depression which interferes with blood supply to the brain. It is caused by violent injury, particularly burns, fractures, or heavy bleeding, or by strong emotions.

### SYMPTOMS

Paleness—hands and nose are cold and clammy, faintness or unconsciousness, breathing that is shallow and irregular, and a pulse that's feeble and rapid.

### FIRST AID

Apply the same First Aid as for fainting except shock is more stubborn and more serious. If there is bleeding, check it, give air, lay the patient with head low, keep them warm, apply heat to arms and limbs, and stimulate cautiously as for fainting.

## BRUISES

### DEFINITION

A bruise is a blow or injury which does not break the skin. (When the skin is broken, these are called wounds.)

### SYMPTOMS

Pain if touched, swelling, and discoloration.

### FIRST AID

Apply either very hot or very cold applications.

## BURNS AND SCALDS

### DEFINITION

Burns are injuries to the skin and tissue caused by excessive dry heat. Scalds are similar injuries caused by moist heat.

*SYMPTOMS*

The surface is blistered or the skin is broken. The danger is from infection, so do not break any blisters.

*FIRST AID*

Use a cloth on which is spread vaseline, olive oil, castor oil, fresh lard or cream, or cold cream to keep the air out. Gauze is probably the best dressing. Moisten it in water or in front of a steaming kettle spout (this will help to disinfect it).

If clothing sticks to a burn, cut around it and leave it there.

Treat burns from alkalis or acids by washing off **as quickly as possible** and counteract the acids with baking soda or a weak ammonia solution—the alkalis with vinegar or lemon juice.

Sunburn is treated much like other burns.

SPRAINS

*DEFINITION*

A sprain is a wrenching, stretching, or tearing of ligaments surrounding a joint (like the ankle or wrist). There may also be slight cracking or breaking of the bones.

*SYMPTOMS*

Pain, stiffness, swelling, and discoloration (the area sprained turns black and blue).

*FIRST AID*

Elevate the joint to relieve the pressure and pain. Apply cloths wrung out of very hot or very cold water or, even better, alternate them every few minutes—this should be kept up for some hours. Good liniments reduce pain. Shock may be present in the patient. A doctor should be called. If forced to use the sprained member, tight bandaging is necessary. After pain and swelling have subsided, a gentle massage may be helpful.

## STRAINS

### *DEFINITION*

A strain is the overstretching of a muscle.

### *SYMPTOMS*

Pain, stiffness, and lameness.

### *FIRST AID*

Get plenty of rest. Rub the area with a good liniment—rub toward the heart. Apply heat.

## THE HEIMLICH MANEUVER

The Heimlich Maneuver can make the difference between life and death for a choking victim. It requires no special training, so anyone—perhaps even you—can save a life.

Choking may occur in a restaurant, at home, or in the field and is more likely to happen during activities such as eating; but young children may also choke on small objects like toy blocks or marbles. Your first impulse may be to slap the sufferer on the back. This is often not a good idea as this is just as likely to drive the blockage further into the throat as it is to dislodge it. The trick is to stay calm. First of all, make sure the victim is actually choking and not having some other breathing problem, like an asthma attack.

Signs of real choking include:

- Inability to speak
- Wheezing, high-pitched cough
- Victim is not breathing
- Victim's skin is turning blue (from lack of oxygen)
- Victim's hand is grabbing at her throat
- Victim falls unconscious

Once you're certain the victim is choking, it's time to take action. First and foremost, stay calm and clear-headed.

Get the victim to a standing position while positioning yourself behind him or her.

Make a fist with one hand and reach around the victim, pressing it up against the victim's abdomen between the bellybutton and the bottom of the ribcage.

Place your thumb on the inside, up against the victim's abdomen, covering your fist with your other hand.

Begin a series of quick, upward thrusts; this should force air from the lungs up through the throat, dislodging the blockage.

Continue with this action until the blockage is expelled through the victim's mouth.

Keep a hold on the victim for a while after dislodging the blockage, as he or she may fall (or already be) unconscious.

If you are alone and you begin to choke, you can perform the Heimlich Maneuver on yourself, but you must act quickly and remain calm. First make a fist of one hand and cover it, clasping it tightly with your other hand. Then press it firmly up against your abdomen between the bellybutton and the bottom of the ribcage.

Perform a series of quick, upward thrusts and this ought to force enough air through the lungs and up through the throat to dislodge the blockage. You may even make use of any sturdy, waist-height object (like the back of a chair or table) by pressing it against your abdomen and thrusting onto the object sharply and forcefully. With any luck this will dislodge the blockage.

## HOW TO TALK TO BOYS

Imagine a scenario where your friend is finally ready to make her move on a guy who she likes, maybe to have lunch with him, to ask him out, or something like that. Now, when she asks you for advice, wouldn't you just love to be the smooth, experienced one who always knows the right thing to say? (Unless, of course, you like the same boy too and want to sabotage your friend.) You probably wish that you could be that sophisticated person, whether it's a matter of just giving advice or talking to the boy yourself. Now, I'm not saying that I am any kind of expert on this . . . but I'm going to give you my advice. When trying to talk to a boy, many girls fall into traps. It's difficult because even if you like a guy, you don't want to put yourself in a vulnerable position by letting him know you have feelings for him if he doesn't like you back.

So, some girls giggle, punctuating their talk with high-pitched squeals. But this only makes their friends want to kill them. Others flirt in such an obvious way that the boy is embarrassed, and all his friends laugh at him. Some girls turn mean or aggressive. Some girls merely clam-up. But very few girls just act like themselves. And this is how you really need to behave.

In short, if you like a guy, or if you just want to get to know a guy better because he seems like a cool person, just be yourself—as corny, or cliché as that may sound. If the guy is as cool a person as you think, then he will respect you for who you are and if he doesn't, then he's not worth your time. And after all, he's not the only boy on the planet.

## HOW TO THROW A SLUMBER PARTY

Who doesn't love a slumber party? But if you want a really good one, some planning is important. Here are just a few thoughts on how to plan and throw a really terrific slumber party.

### *INVITES*

Invites, or invitations, are a little tricky to do but if you do them right, it will be worth it. There is always the question of how many people to invite. Big, ten-people parties are always fun, but in some cases it is better to go with a smaller group. It really all depends on what you are looking for in a party. If you invite more then six people, then be prepared for the fact that people will probably split themselves into little groups. Now, this is sometimes fun, but if you want everyone to hang out together in one group, try not to invite more then five people.

### *AT THE PARTY*

Once you have started the party (and gotten the food), you'll need to have some idea what do to. I don't recommend making a formal plan because, well, what fun is that? But just don't forget that there is a difference between over-planning and being prepared. Decide what you want to do but not in every detail. For example, if you want to watch a movie, then ask your friends what they want to see: chic flic, scarey movie, etc.

*ONE LAST TIP*

Try not to make too big of a mess. If you trash the place, your parents won't appreciate it and it may be quite a long time until they permit another such a bash. But if you do plan to make a big mess, try and have the party at one of your friend's houses, then cleaning up will be someone else's problem!

## THE MATH SLUMBER PARTY

*By Lara L. Brennan*

Once there lived a girl named Abby. She lived in NYC with her little sister Rose. The two girls were the best of friends, so when Rose's seventh birthday came along, fourteen-year-old Abby could not wait to plan it. The girls decided that they wanted to have a math party; after all, who doesn't love math?

"Why don't you do a **pi** theme?" suggested Abby.

"You mean a party about 3.14?" asked Rose.

"No," said Abby. "**Pi** and 3.14 are not the same thing. **Pi** is a never-ending number. 3.14 is just how it is usually expressed. Another cool thing about **pi**," Abby continued, "is that it is an **irrational** number meaning that it cannot be expressed as a **ratio**."

"Wow!" said Rose, "That sounds like a super idea for a party! But, I don't think that there are enough **pi**-related activities for us to do."

"Oh well, that's too bad," agreed Abby.

"But we could go to that awesome math movie that's just come out!" said Rose.

"Good idea!" said Abby. "First we need to figure out how much tickets will cost."

"Great!" shouted Rose enthusiastically. "But how do we do that?"

"Firstly," said Abby, "we need to figure out how many people you want to invite, then we can make a **proportion** or **ratio**."

"I'm not sure what you mean," said Rose.

"Well, you know that the total cost of the event is **dependent** on how many people come because the cost will depend on how many people we need to buy tickets for. This also means that the number of people is **independent** of the cost. No matter how much the tickets cost, the same number of people are still going to be there."

"Oh!" said Rose, "Now I get it! I think that I will invite five and a half friends to the party!"

"Five and a half!" exclaimed Abby, holding back a laugh. "You cant just spilt people in half, you have to have a **natural number**, which is an **integer**, although it's a lot more specific the just an integer because an integer can be positive or negative as long as it is a **whole number** or a number which has no fractions or decimals attached. The difference is that a **natural number** can only be positive."

"Okay then," said Rose. "I'll invite six friends, but don't you think that we should check to make sure that there is enough space in our living room? We'll have six sleeping bags plus ours which makes eight sleeping bags, total."

"Now you're thinking like a mathematician!" said Abby proudly.

So both girls dashed into their living room.

"Okay," said Rose. "First we should get the **perimeter** of the room, right?"

"Wrong." Abby said. "The perimeter is the lengths of all the sides added up. It does not measure the actual space within. I think what you meant to say," Abby continued, "was first we need to find the **area** which measures the actual space inside a shape. You can find the area by multiplying the length of the shape by the width of the shape."

After a quick struggle in finding the tape measure, the girls measured the length and width of the space and then measured the sleeping bags to see how many they could fit in the space that they had. They discovered that not only did they have enough room to fit all eight sleeping bags but that there was room for them to move around, tell secrets, and make hot cocoa and lots of yummy munchies.

The next night at the party, as she watched her little sister and her little friends playing around, Abby noticed lots of math-related stuff at the party. For example, she noticed that at one point, all of the kids were standing in a perfectly straight **line**. She thought it was adorable when she heard Rose and one of her friends named Marie debate the difference between **volume** and **surface area**. She was surprised that both girls knew that **volume** was the length times width times height and that the **surface area** is the **area** of all the surfaces on a three-**dimensional** object.

The next day, after the party ended, both girls were sad that the party was over but now had discovered how to use math in their daily lives in an exciting and fun way!

## A MAD TEA PARTY

*It's often said that tea began as a medicine and then became a beverage, and this is probably true. After all, it is only a mild stimulant. In the Far East, where it originated, the practice of people taking tea together has a long history. Over time, various rites and ceremonies grew up around this communal sipping and slurping; most notably in the Japanese Tea Ceremony, which is tea preparation and guzzling practiced almost as a fine art. In the Western World we reflect some of these formal practices in our own tea drinking, in our tea parties, and four-o'clock-teas. In* Alice In Wonderland, *Lewis Carroll turns any idea of politeness and formality on its head.*

"There was a table set out under a tree in front of the house, and the March Hare and the Hatter were having tea at it: a Dormouse was sitting between them, fast asleep, and the other two were using it as a cushion, resting their elbows on it, and the talking over its head. 'Very uncomfortable for the Dormouse,' thought Alice; 'only, as it's asleep, I suppose it doesn't mind.'

"The table was a large one, but the three were all crowded together at one corner of it: 'No room! No room!' they cried out when they saw Alice coming. 'There's PLENTY of room!' said Alice indignantly, and she sat down in a large arm-chair at one end of the table.

'Have some wine,' the March Hare said in an encouraging tone.

"Alice looked all round the table, but there was nothing on it but tea. 'I don't see any wine,' she remarked.

'There isn't any,' said the March Hare.

'Then it wasn't very civil of you to offer it,' said Alice angrily.

'It wasn't very civil of you to sit down without being invited,' said the March Hare.

'I didn't know it was YOUR table,' said Alice; 'it's laid for a great many more than three.'

'Your hair wants cutting,' said the Hatter. He had been looking at Alice for some time with great curiosity, and this was his first speech.

'You should learn not to make personal remarks,' Alice said with some severity; 'it's very rude.'

"The Hatter opened his eyes very wide on hearing this; but all he SAID was, 'Why is a raven like a writing-desk?'

'Come, we shall have some fun now!' thought Alice. 'I'm glad they've begun asking riddles.—I believe I can guess that,' she added aloud.

'Do you mean that you think you can find out the answer to it?' said the March Hare.

'Exactly so,' said Alice.

'Then you should say what you mean,' the March Hare went on.

'I do,' Alice hastily replied; 'at least—at least I mean what I say—that's the same thing, you know.'

'Not the same thing a bit!' said the Hatter. 'You might just as well say that "I see what I eat" is the same thing as "I eat what I see"!'

'You might just as well say,' added the March Hare, 'that "I like what I get" is the same thing as "I get what I like"!'

'You might just as well say,' added the Dormouse, who seemed to be talking in his sleep, 'that "I breathe when I sleep" is the same thing as "I sleep when I breathe"!'

'It IS the same thing with you,' said the Hatter, and here the conversation dropped, and the party sat silent for a minute, while Alice thought over all she could remember about ravens and writing-desks, which wasn't much.

"The Hatter was the first to break the silence. 'What day of the month is it?' he said, turning to Alice: he had taken his watch out of his pocket, and was looking at it uneasily, shaking it every now and then, and holding it to his ear.

"Alice considered a little, and then said 'The fourth.'

'Two days wrong!' sighed the Hatter. 'I told you butter wouldn't suit the works!' he added looking angrily at the March Hare.

'It was the BEST butter,' the March Hare meekly replied.

'Yes, but some crumbs must have got in as well,' the Hatter grumbled: 'you shouldn't have put it in with the bread-knife.'

"The March Hare took the watch and looked at it gloomily: then he dipped it into his cup of tea, and looked at it again: but he could think of nothing better to say than his first remark, 'It was the BEST butter, you know.'

"Alice had been looking over his shoulder with some curiosity. 'What a funny watch!' she remarked. 'It tells the day of the month, and doesn't tell what o'clock it is!'

'Why should it?' muttered the Hatter. 'Does YOUR watch tell you what year it is?'

'Of course not,' Alice replied very readily: 'but that's because it stays the same year for such a long time together.'

'Which is just the case with MINE,' said the Hatter.

"Alice felt dreadfully puzzled. The Hatter's remark seemed to have no sort of meaning in it, and yet it was certainly English. 'I don't quite understand you,' she said, as politely as she could.

'The Dormouse is asleep again,' said the Hatter, and he poured a little hot tea upon its nose.

"The Dormouse shook its head impatiently, and said, without opening its eyes, 'Of course, of course; just what I was going to remark myself.'

'Have you guessed the riddle yet?' the Hatter said, turning to Alice again.

'No, I give it up,' Alice replied: 'that's the answer?'

'I haven't the slightest idea,' said the Hatter.

'Nor I,' said the March Hare.

Alice sighed wearily. 'I think you might do something better with the time,' she said, 'than waste it in asking riddles that have no answers.'

'If you knew Time as well as I do,' said the Hatter, 'you wouldn't talk about wasting IT. It's HIM.'

'I don't know what you mean,' said Alice.

'Of course you don't!' the Hatter said, tossing his head contemptuously. 'I dare say you never even spoke to Time!'

'Perhaps not,' Alice cautiously replied: 'but I know I have to beat time when I learn music.'

'Ah! that accounts for it,' said the Hatter. 'He won't stand beating. Now, if you only kept on good terms with him, he'd do almost anything you liked with the clock. For instance, suppose it were nine o'clock in the morning, just time to begin lessons: you'd only have to whisper a hint to Time, and round goes the clock in a twinkling! Half-past one, time for dinner!'

('I only wish it was,' the March Hare said to itself in a whisper.)

'That would be grand, certainly,' said Alice thoughtfully: 'but then— I shouldn't be hungry for it, you know.'

'Not at first, perhaps,' said the Hatter: 'but you could keep it to half-past one as long as you liked.'

'Is that the way YOU manage?' Alice asked.

"The Hatter shook his head mournfully. 'Not I!' he replied. 'We quarrelled last March—just before HE went mad, you know—' (pointing with his tea spoon at the March Hare,) '—it was at the great concert given by the Queen of Hearts, and I had to sing

"Twinkle, twinkle, little bat!
How I wonder what you're at!"

You know the song, perhaps?'

'I've heard something like it,' said Alice.

'It goes on, you know,' the Hatter continued, 'in this way:—

"Up above the world you fly,
Like a tea-tray in the sky.
Twinkle, twinkle—"'

"Here the Dormouse shook itself, and began singing in its sleep 'Twinkle, twinkle, twinkle, twinkle—' and went on so long that they had to pinch it to make it stop.

'Well, I'd hardly finished the first verse,' said the Hatter, 'when the Queen jumped up and bawled out, "He's murdering the time! Off with his head!"'

'How dreadfully savage!' exclaimed Alice.

'And ever since that,' the Hatter went on in a mournful tone, 'he won't do a thing I ask! It's always six o'clock now.'

"A bright idea came into Alice's head. 'Is that the reason so many tea-things are put out here?' she asked.

'Yes, that's it,' said the Hatter with a sigh: 'it's always tea-time, and we've no time to wash the things between whiles.'

'Then you keep moving round, I suppose?' said Alice.

'Exactly so,' said the Hatter: 'as the things get used up.'

'But what happens when you come to the beginning again?' Alice ventured to ask.

'Suppose we change the subject,' the March Hare interrupted, yawning. 'I'm getting tired of this. I vote the young lady tells us a story.'

'I'm afraid I don't know one,' said Alice, rather alarmed at the proposal.

'Then the Dormouse shall!' they both cried. 'Wake up, Dormouse!' And they pinched it on both sides at once.

"The Dormouse slowly opened his eyes. 'I wasn't asleep,' he said in a hoarse, feeble voice: 'I heard every word you fellows were saying.'

'Tell us a story!' said the March Hare.

'Yes, please do!' pleaded Alice.

'And be quick about it,' added the Hatter, 'or you'll be asleep again before it's done.'

'Once upon a time there were three little sisters,' the Dormouse began in a great hurry; 'and their names were Elsie, Lacie, and Tillie; and they lived at the bottom of a well—'

'What did they live on?' said Alice, who always took a great interest in questions of eating and drinking.

'They lived on treacle,' said the Dormouse, after thinking a minute or two.

'They couldn't have done that, you know,' Alice gently remarked; 'they'd have been ill.'

'So they were,' said the Dormouse; 'VERY ill.'

"Alice tried to fancy to herself what such an extraordinary ways of living would be like, but it puzzled her too much, so she went on: 'But why did they live at the bottom of a well?'

'Take some more tea,' the March Hare said to Alice, very earnestly.

'I've had nothing yet,' Alice replied in an offended tone, 'so I can't take more.'

'You mean you can't take LESS,' said the Hatter: 'it's very easy to take MORE than nothing.'

'Nobody asked YOUR opinion,' said Alice.

'Who's making personal remarks now?' the Hatter asked triumphantly.

"Alice did not quite know what to say to this: so she helped herself to some tea and bread-and-butter, and then turned to the Dormouse, and repeated her question. 'Why did they live at the bottom of a well?'

"The Dormouse again took a minute or two to think about it, and then said, 'It was a treacle-well.'

'There's no such thing!' Alice was beginning very angrily, but the Hatter and the March Hare went 'Sh! sh!' and the Dormouse sulk-ily remarked, 'If you can't be civil, you'd better finish the story for yourself.'

'No, please go on!' Alice said very humbly; 'I won't interrupt again. I dare say there may be ONE.'

'One, indeed!' said the Dormouse indignantly. However, he con-sented to go on. 'And so these three little sisters—they were learning to draw, you know—'

'What did they draw?' said Alice, quite forgetting her promise.

'Treacle,' said the Dormouse, without considering at all this time.

'I want a clean cup,' interrupted the Hatter: 'let's all move one place on.'

"He moved on as he spoke, and the Dormouse followed him: the March Hare moved into the Dormouse's place, and Alice rather unwillingly took the place of the March Hare. The Hatter was the only one who got any advantage from the change: and Alice was a good deal worse off than before, as the March Hare had just upset the milk-jug into his plate.

"Alice did not wish to offend the Dormouse again, so she began very cautiously: 'But I don't understand. Where did they draw the treacle from?'

'You can draw water out of a water-well,' said the Hatter; 'so I should think you could draw treacle out of a treacle-well—eh, stupid?'

'But they were IN the well,' Alice said to the Dormouse, not choosing to notice this last remark.

'Of course they were', said the Dormouse; '—well in.'

"This answer so confused poor Alice, that she let the Dormouse go on for some time without interrupting it.

'They were learning to draw,' the Dormouse went on, yawning and rubbing its eyes, for it was getting very sleepy; 'and they drew all manner of things—everything that begins with an M—'

'Why with an M?' said Alice.

'Why not?' said the March Hare.

"Alice was silent.

"The Dormouse had closed its eyes by this time, and was going off into a doze; but, on being pinched by the Hatter, it woke up again with a little shriek, and went on: '—that begins with an M, such as mouse-traps, and the moon, and memory, and muchness— you know you say things are "much of a muchness"—did you ever see such a thing as a drawing of a muchness?'

'Really, now you ask me,' said Alice, very much confused, 'I don't think—'

'Then you shouldn't talk,' said the Hatter.

"This piece of rudeness was more than Alice could bear: she got up in great disgust, and walked off; the Dormouse fell asleep instantly, and neither of the others took the least notice of her going, though she looked back once or twice, half hoping that they would call after her: the last time she saw them, they were trying to put the Dormouse into the teapot.

'At any rate I'll never go THERE again!' said Alice as she picked her way through the wood. 'It's the stupidest tea-party I ever was at in all my life!'"

## HOW TO PUT TOGETHER AN OUTFIT

"How do you put together an outfit?" or "What shall I wear today?" Ahh, the eternal questions. Putting together a good outfit requires you to know what sort of affect you're looking for. Try to see yourself as others will. But there's really a lot less to this than many people think.

Keep it clean. The clothes you wear should be clean and comfortable so that you can look and feel your best.

Don't be afraid of color. If you think you have a good idea, don't hold back. Give it a try. But if you feel as though you are in a costume, especially compared to what the other girls at school are wearing, just relax. If you behave as though your outfit is no good, it's likely that's what others will think too.

Think about where you are going. If you are simply going out to the park to hang out with your friends, you might want to wear something that will not get dirty easily, or at least something that will not show the dirt. If you are going to a more-formal occasion, like a wedding, then you really ought to make the effort to show some respect and dress up a little.

Be mindful of school rules. Sometimes your school dress code can be a tiny, little bit annoying…sometimes, but still, it's a good idea to follow the rules

## HOW TO BUILD A FORT OUT OF CUSHIONS

*By Jennifer McCartney*

Couch cushions aren't just for sitting on! Most couch cushions can be easily removed and used to create the fort of your dreams! Especially good for rainy and snowy days when you're stuck inside—couch cushion forts are simply the best. Try leaning two cushions together to make a tent. Try combining the cushions from more than one couch to make lean-tos, castles, caves, and comfortable hideaways. If you want a proper roof, balance one cushion upright and place another cushion across it, using the arm of the couch as a base on the other side. Try draping a blanket across the entrance for extra privacy. Think big or think small—it's all up to you! Use your imagination. Is your couch cushion cave located underwater? In the clouds? Are you living in a castle in medieval times, or are you a secret time-traveling spy from the future, living in your secret lair? Who are you going to invite into your fort? Or is it a special place just for you? Anything goes! Once your fort is ready for occupation, make sure to remember the blankets from your bed, your stuffed animals, and your favorite book. The best part is at the end of the day there's no mess! You can pop those cushions back on the couch and start over again tomorrow.


## HOW TO SPEAK SIGN LANGUAGE

*By Ernest Thompson Seton*

Do you know Sign Language?

If not, do you realize that Sign Language is an established mode of communication in all parts of the world without regard to native speech?

Do you know that it is so refined and complete that sermons and lectures are given in it every day, to those who cannot hear?

Do you know that it is as old as the hills and is largely used in all public schools? And yet, when I ask boys and girls this question, "Do you use Sign Language?" they nearly always say, "No."

Why should you talk in Sign Language? There are many reasons.

It makes conversation easy in places when you must not speak aloud.

It is a means of far-signalling much quicker than semaphore or other *spelling* codes.

It will enable you to talk when there is too much noise to be heard, as across the noisy streets.

It makes it possible to talk to a deaf person.

It is a wonderful developer of observation.

It is a simple means of talking to someone of another nationality whose language you do not understand. This indeed is its greatest merit. It is *universal*. It deals not with words but with ideas that are common to all mankind. It is therefore a kind of Esperanto (universal language)

So much for its advantages. What are its weaknesses?

It is useless in the dark.

It will not serve on the telephone or computer.

It can scarcely be written.

In its pure form it will not give new proper names.

To meet the last two we have expedients, as will be seen, but the first two are insurmountable difficulties.

Remember then you want to learn Sign Language because it is *silent, far-reaching*, and the one *universal language*.

Since it deals fundamentally with ideas, we avoid words and letters, but for proper names it is very necessary to know the one-hand manual alphabet.

Here are some of the better-known signs. Each girl will probably find that she already knows and uses them often.

*You* (pointing at the person)

*Me* (tapping one's chest)

*My, mine, yours, possession, etc.* Hold out the closed fist, thumb up, and swing it down a little so thumb points forward.

*Yes* (nod). When far off, make your right hand, with all fingers closed except index and thumb which are straight and touching at top, advance, bend toward the left side as though bowing, then return and straighten again.

*No* (head shake). When too far for that to be seen, hold the closed right hand in front of the body, then sweep it, outward and downward. At the same time turn the palm up as though throwing something away.

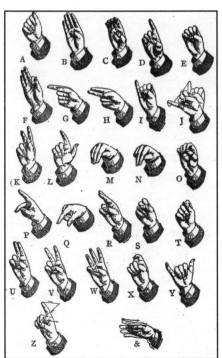

*Eat* (throw the flat hand several times past the mouth in a curve)

*Drink* (hold the right hand as though holding a cup near the mouth and tip it up)

*Sleep* (lay the right cheek on the right flat hand)

*Look* (flat hand over eyes)

*Look there* (point and look in same direction)

*Touch* (reach out and touch with index)

*Listen* (flat hand behind ear)

*Whisper* (silently move lips, holding flat hand at one side of mouth)

*Silence* or *hush* (forefinger across lips)

*I will not listen* (hold flat hands on ears)

*I will not look* (cover eyes with hands)
*Taste* (lay finger on lip)
*Smell* (hold palm to nose)
*That tastes good* (smack the lips)
*The food was good* (pat the stomach)
*Bad taste* (grimace and spitting out)
*Bad smell* (hold the nose)
Thus *"Will you eat?"* would be a *Question, you eat,* but *"Have you eaten?"* would be, *Question, you eat, finished.*

*Drinking* (lift right hand to mouth as though it held a glass)
*Smoking* (make as though holding a pipe and drawing)
*Paint* (use flat right as a brush to paint flat left)
*Shave* (use finger or thumb on face as a razor)
*Wash* (revolve hands on each other as in washing)
*Bend* (with right hand bend left index)
*Break* (with fists touching, make as though to bend a stick, then swing the fists apart)
*Write* (make the action with index)
*Strike* (strike down with fist)
*Fighting* (make the fists menace each other)
*Set it afire* (sign match, and then thrust it forward)
*Drive horses* (work the two fists, side by side)
*Finished* or *done* (hold out the flat left hand palm to the right, then with flat right hand, chop down past the ends of the left fingers)
*Search me* (hold the coat flaps open in each hand)
*Swim* (strike out with flat hands)
*Dive* (flat hands together moved in a curve forward and down)
*Will you come swimming?* (first and second fingers raised and spread, others closed)
*Good* (nod and clap hands)
*Bad* (shake head and grimace)
*"Very"* or *"very much,"* is made by striking the right fist down past the knuckles of the left without quite touching them, the left being held still.

*Hot* (wet middle finger in mouth, reach it forward, and jerk it back)
*Cold* (fists near shoulder and shaken)
*Good-bye* (hand high, flat, palm down, fingers wagged all together)

*Thank you* (a slight bow, smile, and hand-salute, made by drawing flat hand a few inches forward and downward palm up)

*Surrender* (both hands raised high and flat to show no weapons)

*I am thinking it over* (forefinger on right brow and eyes raised)

*I forgot* (touch forehead with all right finger tips, then draw flat hand past eyes once and shake head)

*I wind him around my finger* (make action with right thumb and index around left index)

*I have him under my thumb* (press firmly down with top of right thumb)

*Sleepy* (put a fist in each eye)

*Bellyache* (with hands clasped across the belly)

*Sick* (a grimace and a limp dropping of hands)

*Go* (move hand forward, palm first)

*Come* (draw hand toward one's self, palm in)

*Hurry* (same as *come*, but the hand quickly and energetically moved several times)

*Come for a moment* (hand held out back down, fingers closed except first, which is hooked and straightened quickly several times)

*Stop* (flat hand held up, palm forward)

*Gently* or *Go easy* (like "stop," but hand gently waved from side to side)

*Get up* (raise flat hand sharply, palm upward)

*Sit down* (drop flat hand sharply, palm down)

*Rub it out* (quickly shake flat hand from side to side, palm forward)

*Up* (forefinger pointed and moved upward)

*Down* (ditto downward)

*Way* or *road* (hold both flat hands nearly side by side, palms up, but put the right one nearer the breast. Then alternately lift them forward and draw them back to indicate track or feet traveling)

*Forward* (swing index finger forward and down in a curve)

*Backward* (jerk left hand over shoulder)

*Across* (hold left hand out flat, palm down, run right index across it)

*Over* and *above* (hold out flat left hand, palm down, and above it hold right hand the same)

*Under* (reverse or foregoing)

*It's in my pocket* (slap pocket with flat hand)

*I send you a kiss* (kiss finger tips and move hand in graceful sweep toward person)

*I pray* (clasped hands held up)

*I am afraid*, or *surrender* (hold up both flat hands palm forward)

*I forget* (slowly shake head, and brush away something in air, near the nose)

*I am seeking* (looking about and pointing finger in same directions)

*I have my doubts* (slowly swing head from side to side)

*You surprise me* (flat hand on open mouth)

*Connivance* (winking one eye)

*Puzzled* (scratch the head)

*Crazy* (tap forehead with index then draw a circle with it)

*Despair* (pulling the hair)

*Weeping* (with index finger at each eye, trace course of tears)

*Friendship* (hands clasped)

*Threatening* (fist shaken at person)

*Warning* (forefinger gently shaken at a slight angle toward person)

*Scorn* (turning away and throwing an imaginary handful of sand toward person)

*Insolent defiance* (thumb to nose tips, fingers fully spread)

*Indifference* (a shoulder shrug)

*Ignorance* (a shrug and headshake combined)

*Arrogant* (indicate swelled head)

*Pompous* (indicate a big chest)

*Incredulity* (expose white of eye with finger, as though proving no green there)

*Shame on you* (right forefinger drawn across left toward person several times)

*You make me ashamed* (cover eyes and face with hands)

*Mockery* (stick tongue at person)

*Disdain* (snap fingers toward person)

*Applause* (silently make as though clapping hands)

*Victory* (hold one hand high above head as though waving hat)

*He is cross* (forefinger crossed and level)

*Fool* or *ass* (a thumb in each ear, flat hands up)

*Cutthroat* (draw index finger across throat)

*I am no fool* (tap one side of the nose)

*Joke* (rub side of nose with index finger)

*Upon my honor* (with forefingers make a cross over heart)

*I beg of you* (flat hands held tight together and upright)

*Do you think me simple?* (forefinger laid on side of nose)

*Will you?* or, *Is it so?* (eyebrows raised and slight bow made)

*Bar up, fins,* or *I claim exemption* (cross second finger of right hand on first finger and hold hand up)

*Poverty* (both hands turned flat forward near trouser pockets)

*Bribe* (hand held hollow up behind the back)

*Give me* (hold out open flat hand pulling it back a little to finish)

*I give you* (the same, but push forward to finish)

*Pay* (hand held out half open, forefinger and thumb rubbed together)

*Give me my bill* (same, then make motion of writing)

*Church* (hands clasped, fingers in, but index fingers up and touching)

*Revolver* (hold out right fist with index extended and thumb up)

*Gun* or *shooting* (hold hands as in aiming a gun)

*Match* (make the sign of striking a match on the thigh)

*Knife* (first and second fingers of right hand used as to whittle first finger of left)

*House* (hold the flat hands together like a roof)

*Pistol* (making barrel with left hand, stock and hammer with-right, snap right index on thumb)

*Query.* The sign for *Question*—that is, "I am asking you a question," "I want to know"—is much used and important. Hold up the right hand toward the person, palm forward, fingers open, slightly curved and spread. Wave the hand gently by wrist action from side to side. It is used before, and sometimes after, all questions. If you are very near, merely raise the eyebrows.

The following are needed in asking questions:

*How Many?* or *How much?*

First the *Question* sign, then hold the left hand open, curved, palm up, fingers spread. Then with right digit, quickly tap each finger of left hand in succession, closing it back toward the left hand palm, beginning with the little finger.

*What?* What are you doing? What do you want? What is it? First give *Question*, then hold right hand palm down, fingers slightly bent and separated, and, pointing forward, throw it about a foot from right to left several times, drawing an arc upward.

*When?* If seeking a definite answer as to a length of time, make signs for *Question, How much*, and then specify time by a sign for hours, days, etc. When asking in general, *"When"* for a date, hold the left index extended and vertical, other fingers and thumb closed, make a circle round left

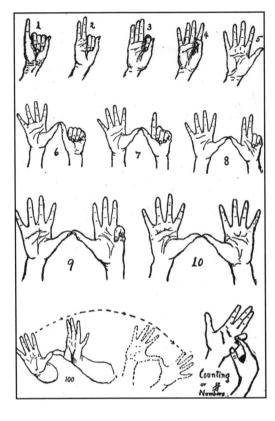

index tip with tip of extended right index, other fingers and thumb closed; and when the index reaches the starting point, stop it, and point at tip of left index (what point of shadow?).

*Where?* (What direction) *Question,* then with forefinger sweep the horizon in a succession of bounds, a slight pause at the bottom of each.

*Which?* *Question,* then hold left hand in front of you with palm toward you, fingers to right and held apart; place the end of the right forefinger on that of left forefinger, and then draw it down across the other fingers.

*Why?* Make the sign for *Question,* but do it very slowly.

*Who?* *Question,* and then draw with the right forefinger a small circle six inches in front of the mouth.

It takes a good-sized dictionary to give all the signs in use, and a dictionary you must have, if you want to become an expert.

A very pretty sign is given as follows: First, give the *Question* sign, then make an incomplete ring of your right forefinger and thumb, raise them in a sweep until above your head, then bring the ring straight down to your heart. This is the Indian way of asking, "Is the sun shining in your heart?"—that is, "Are you happy?" Your answer will be made by the right hand and arm standing up straight, then bowing toward the left, followed by a sharp stroke of the right fist knuckles past those of the left fist without their touching, which means: "Yes, the sun shines in my heart *heap strong.*"

## HOW DOES YOUR GARDEN GROW?

*By David M. Hunter*

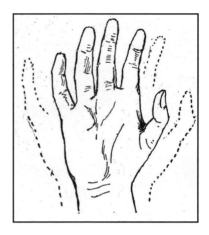

QUERY SIGN

For the beginner gardner, I recommend a very small garden to start with because it is well to undertake only that which can be easily handled and managed thoroughly. There is joy in the contemplation of a perfect work, even though it is on a small scale, that never comes from a more ambitious undertaking imperfectly carried out. Better six square feet of well-tilled, weedless, thrifty garden than an acre poorly cultivated and full of weeds.

Anyone who wants to make a garden will naturally ask certain questions. If she has the ground, if she knows already where her garden is to be placed, the next thing, perhaps, that she will wish to know is what tools will be needed. Then follows the way to treat the soil in order to prepare it for planting the seeds. After that comes the question of seeds and the way to plant them. Finally, the cultivation of the crops until they are ready to be gathered must be understood.

## TOOLS

Not many tools will be needed, but some seem to be indispensable. I would suggest:

A spading fork. Some like a long-handled fork, others prefer a short-handled one.

A hoe.

A garden or iron-toothed rake.

A hand weeder of some kind.

A shovel.

In addition to these tools every gardener will find it necessary to have a line for making straight rows. This should be at least the length of the longest dimension of the garden and white so it may be easily seen. There should be two pegs to stick it in with. I should add a board about ten inches wide with straight edges and as long as the bed is wide, and a pointed stick.

## THE PREPARATION OF THE SEED BED

The first thing to do, after having determined the location of your garden, is to measure your bed. If you have a single bed, one twelve feet long by six feet wide is enough to start with. Many people prefer, however, to have two beds, each three feet wide by twelve feet long with a narrow path between. The reason for laying out the ground in two beds is that it will be easier to reach the whole bed from either side without stepping or kneeling on the cultivated soil. All cultivation can be done from the paths.

*The soil* for flower beds needs most careful preparation. The bed should be dug out to a depth of two feet, and if the soil is clay, two feet six inches. In the latter case, put broken stones, cinders, or gravel on the bottom for drainage. The soil should be a mixture of one-half good sandy loam, one-fourth leaf mould, or muck that has been left out all winter. Mix these thoroughly together before filling the beds. You may sprinkle wood ashes over the beds and rake them in before planting. This is to sweeten the soil.

*Fertilizer.* Next in order comes the enriching of this plot of ground by spreading a good coating of fertilizer. This done, proceed to fork the whole piece over, thrusting the spading fork into the ground its full length each time, and turning the forkful of earth so that the fertilizer will be covered and not lie on top of the ground.

When the spading has been done, then use your rake and rake the bed very well. Rake until the earth in the beds is finely pulverized and until the whole bed is as level as you can make it.

Now construct your central, or dividing, path, throwing the soil moved on the beds on either side. To do this you will need a shovel.

Next, define, or limit, your beds, making the sides and ends as straight as possible. You ought now to have two rectangular beds, each three feet by twelve feet, with a narrow path separating them all ready to put the seeds in. It would be a good thing to have your beds raised a little, two or three inches above the general level of the surrounding earth. This will help them drain.

## SEEDS

Use great care in the selection of seeds because it is a bitter disappointment and a discouraging experience to find that after all your labor your seeds are worthless. It would be well to test a sample of your seeds to determine their germinating power. If you have a reliable friend from whom you can secure your seeds, you are fortunate, but if you must purchase at the dealer by all means patronize one of established reputation.

For the first garden I would plant lettuce, radishes, beets and beans in one of the beds. The other bed may be devoted to flowers.

## PLANTING

Your beds are now supposed to be all ready for the seeds. That is to say, they are shaped and graded and raked fine. The next thing to do is to lay your board across the bed, with one edge six inches from the edge of the bed. Then stand on the board and with a pointed stick make a shallow furrow on each side of the board close to the board. Here I would plant the lettuce. It is desirable to have the seeds evenly and not too thickly distributed in the shallow furrows. One way of accomplishing this is by mixing your seeds with some very fine wood ashes in a bowl and spreading the mixed ashes and seeds along the furrows. A better way, I think, in the case of a small quantity of seeds, would be to place each seed at a proper distance from the others. This distance will vary according to the size of the full-grown heads of lettuce. The smaller varieties might stand six inches apart, while the largest ones would need to be twice that distance or more.

Having planted your lettuce seeds, turn your board over carefully twice. That will bring it into position for two more rows of vegetables. Stand on the board again and proceed as before, making two shallow furrows with a pointed stick. Here I would plant the radish seeds. These may be sown more thickly, for the reason that as soon as the radishes become large enough to eat they may be pulled out, leaving room for the rest of the radishes to develop.

Having planted your radish seeds, repeat the preceding operations, making two furrows again, this time for beet seeds. These may also be sown thickly. The plants may be thinned out afterward. The small plants that are pulled out will make excellent greens. When the thinning is completed, the remaining plants should stand from four to six inches apart, according to variety; some beets are much larger than others.

The rest of the bed devote to string or butter beans. You will have left for these a space of eighty-eight inches, or a little more than seven feet. The rows of beans must be farther apart than the other vegetables you have planted. Two feet between the rows is not too much. You will have space enough for three rows. Measure from your last row of beets one foot six inches at each side of your bed. Now stretch your line across your bed at this distance from the beets, then with a hoe make a furrow close to the line. This furrow should be two inches deep at least—much deeper, you see, than the shallow furrows for the smaller seeds. Having made this furrow, measure two feet from it on each side of the bed and place your line at this point and make a furrow as before. Repeat the process for a third furrow. You should now have left a space of eighteen inches between your last furrow and the end of the bed. Into these three furrows place the beans, spacing them equally.

Your seeds are now all in. At this juncture take your rake and cover the seeds, leaving the whole bed level and smooth.

There is nothing more to be done now except to leave these seeds to the forces of nature, to the darkness and the moisture and the warmth of their earthy bed. They are put to bed not that they may sleep, but in order to wake. Soon the delicate shoots will begin to appear above the ground, and with them will also appear the shoots of many weeds whose seeds were in the soil. These weeds constitute a call to your next operation.


## CULTIVATION

Declare war on the weeds. Use your hand weeder between the rows of smaller vegetables and let no weed escape. If they are in the rows so near to the seedlings that you cannot us the weeder without danger to the delicate little plants that you are attending, then employ your fingers.

For a time you may use the hoe or rake between the rows of beans, but even here near the paths themselves the weeder or hands are preferred.

There is one caution that old gardeners give which is not to work among beans when they are wet with dew or rain for fear of "rust." Wait until the sun has dried the foliage.

Frequent and thorough cultivation not only destroys the weeds, thus giving your vegetables a better chance and giving your garden a tidy, well-kept appearance, but it keeps the soil loose and forms a sort of mulch whereby moisture is conserved. The dryer the season, the greater the need for cultivation.

It may seem to you that you are obliged to wait long and spend a good deal of labor without results, but when you have for breakfast some cool, crisp radishes and for dinner a head of fresh lettuce, and later a dish of sweet, luscious beets or a mess of string beans, you will feel well repaid.

Let us now turn our attention to the other bed, in which you are to grow flowers. This may be treated as a sort of background for the vegetable bed. To do this, let the rows of plants run the other way. That is to say, lengthwise of the bed instead of across. It is assumed that the ground has been treated as in the case of the vegetable bed.

When you have accomplished this work of preparation set your line six inches from the side of the bed nearest your vegetables, or the patch between the two beds. Make a shallow furrow the full length of the bed with your pointed stick. In this furrow, sow your flower seeds of some low-growing plant such as *sweet alyssum*. Then move your line back one foot toward the other side of the bed. Here you should place some taller plants, such as *asters*. The aster plants should have been raised in the house, or purchased from some grower. Again move your line one foot nearer the rear margin of your bed and in this row plant your tallest plants. *Dahlias* or *cosmos* would be very effective. You must get the roots for the dahlias somewhere. Cosmos is planted from seeds. In planting the dahlias it would be well to dig a hole for each plant so deep that when the root is set it will be two or three inches below the surface of the ground. Good results will be obtained if you put a handful or two of fertilizer in the hole and sprinkle a little soil over it before putting in the roots.

I have mentioned these particular plants simply as specimens. Other choices may be made. But whatever the selection, two things should be kept in mind. First, the rows should contain plants that vary in height, the lowest being placed in the front row, the tallest at the back; and second, plants should be chosen that will be in bloom at the same time, for at least a part of the season.

If your work has been well done you ought to have a small bed of vegetables, thrifty, in straight rows, well cultivated, clean, and in back of that, looking from the side, another bed if flowering plants that should be a delight to the eye, especially the eye of the possessor and maker. Of course, the beds will not present this perfect appearance for a long time because as the vegetables are used the beds will show where the vegetables have been removed. It should be mentioned, however, that it is possible to have more than one planting of radishes and lettuce in a season, and these may be replaced after the first planting has been used.

There are many satisfactions in gardening. The intimacy with nature is one of them. To be with growing things through all the stages of their growth, in all weathers and all hours of the day, gives a quiet pleasure that is a healing and soothing influence. To produce something so valuable, so necessary as food by one's own exertion and care confers true dignity and a sense of worth upon one self. To eat what one has raised oneself adds a special flavor to it.

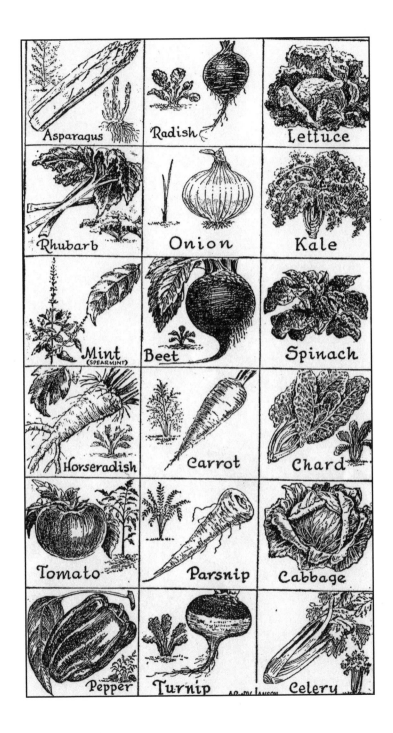

Strawberry

Watermelon

3 leaflet
Raspberry

Early Yellow
Summer
Crook-
neck

white
bush
Squashes

5 Leaflets
Blackberry

Cucumber

Currants

Cantaloupe

Gooseberries

Pumpkin

vine
Grapes

Pole
vine
Gourd

# APPENDIX

# RESOURCES FOR ADVENTUROUS GIRLS

1. **Awesome Adventure Women**—www.aawonline.com. "Awesome Adventure Women was founded in 2005 by Michelle Halbsgut. Her passion for the outdoors and adventure inspired her to form an adventure group for women who want to try new activities, challenge themselves, or simply get out and enjoy the outdoors with like-minded women. Whether they are a beginner, novice, or expert at the skill, women between the age of eighteen and one hundred and eighteen are welcome."

2. **Adventures for Women**—www.adventuresforwomen.org. "Adventures for Women is a nonprofit organization and one of the few "women only" outdoor clubs in the U.S. that brings women of all ages and abilities together to share adventures and camaraderie, learn new skills, develop confidence, and gain new insights and experiences."

3. **Adventure Women Inc.**—www.adventurewomen.com. "Celebrating its twenty-seventh year, AdventureWomen, Inc. has been a pioneer in women's vacations and adventure travel since 1982. Adventure vacations are geared toward women over thirty traveling solo or with sisters, mothers, daughters, and friends."

4. **American Heritage Girls**—www.ahgonline.org. "American Heritage Girls was founded in 1995 by a group of parents wanting a wholesome scouting program for their daughters with a Judeo-Christian focus. The nonprofit organization is dedicated to the mission of building women of integrity through service to God, family, community, and country through its merit badge programs, service projects, girl leadership opportunities, and outdoor experiences to its members."

5. **Call of the Wild**—www.callwild.com. "Call of the Wild began in 1978 and is now the world's longest-running women's adventure travel company. Women-only trips range from active vacations to beginner or challenging backpacking in the wilderness."

6. **Frontier Girls**—www.frontiergirls.com. "Just two years old, the mission of the Frontier Girls is to raise women of honor to be the mothers and leaders of the future through life skills, leadership, character-building, teamwork, and service to others. The Frontier Girls program seeks to restore a focus on good moral character, patriotism, community service, and a love of learning."

7. **Girls Incorporated**—www.girlsinc.org. "Girls Incorporated is a national nonprofit youth organization dedicated to inspiring all girls to be strong, smart, and bold. With roots dating to 1864, Girls Inc. has provided vital educational programs to millions of American girls, particularly those in high-risk, underserved areas. Today, innovative programs help girls confront subtle societal messages about their value and potential and prepare them to lead successful, independent, and fulfilling lives."

8. **Girl Scouts of the USA**—www.girlscouts.org. "Girl Scouts of the USA is the world's preeminent organization dedicated solely to girls where they build character and skills for success in the real world. In partnership with committed adult volunteers, girls develop qualities that will serve them all their lives, like leadership, strong values, social conscience, and conviction about their own potential and self-worth."

9. **Hardy Girls Healthy Women**—www.hardygirlshealthywomen. org. "Hardy Girls Healthy Women (HGHW) is a nonprofit organization dedicated to the health and well-being of girls and women. Our vision is that all girls and women experience equality, independence, and safety in their everyday lives. To that end, our mission is to create opportunities, develop programs, and provide services that empower them."

10. **Top Tips for Girls**—www.toptipsforgirls.com. "Every woman has a handy stash of top tips she's worked out for herself to make life easier. These are little tricks we do almost unconsciously, but we all have our own arsenal, rarely thinking to share. Top Tips for Girls is a fabulous way of sharing our own hard-learned tips on everything from dating to technology. It's a practical, speedy resource with all tips short and to the point."